Thirty-one values clarification strategies
for daily living

Meeting
yourself
halfway

SIDNEY B. SIMON, ED.D.

ARGUS COMMUNICATIONS
1974
NILES, ILLINOIS
60648

Library of Congress Catalog Card Number: 74-19589
International Standard Book Number: 0-913592-30-7

Argus Communications
7440 Natchez Avenue
Niles, IL 60648

THIS BOOK IS DEDICATED
to all those people who have been my teachers
in values clarification.
Louis E. Raths was the first
and the most profound influence
on everything I know in this area.

Merrill Harmin
of Southern Illinois University,
my long-time friend and colleague,
has been an almost-20-year force
in making this work grow within me.

Howard Kirschenbaum,
Director of the National Humanistic
Education Center,
ten-year-long friend and colleague,
has contributed much
to the whole humanistic education movement
and equally much to me, personally.

Then there are the thousands of unnamed students,
workshop attenders, colleagues, and friends
who have etched their own lives
into this book.

They have all been my teachers,
and I will be eternally grateful to them.

Contents

more

Preface

*31 days—31 ways
to meet yourself*

Please don't just read this book. It is a book to be experienced, to be lived.

It is different from books which are meant, merely, to entertain or to give information. This book will try to help all of us live better, more beautiful lives.

So few of us ever reach our magnificent potential. We putter along on ten or fifteen percent of the enormous capacity we have, a capacity to love, to feel, to take risks, to simply enjoy!

But these days we know so much more about what can be done to enhance our own lives. We can become the self we fantasize. The sky is the limit. There seems to be no limit to the Self.

31 days. 31 ways to meet yourself. Getting to know all that you can become is a slow and deliberate process. The strategies in this book, these experiences, these happenings, have been developed over many years through my work with tens of thousands of teachers and students. I sincerely believe that they can help you as they have so many others, to meet your real self, a self grounded in reality, and flourishing in joy. It is a chance to be reborn again, and to soar as brightly as a shooting star.

The strategies found between the covers of this book are intriguing and fascinating and delightful. Rarely will they be threatening or encountering or embarrassing. Many of the strategies involve an "ongoing" process, and some will be more helpful than others.

My suggestion is that you try one—only one—strategy each day for a month. This means, of course, that some of the "ongoing" activities will be interrupted. This will benefit you most if, after having experienced the 31 strategies over 31 days, you return to pursue in depth those "ongoing" activities that seemed most revealing and beneficial.

Remember, just reading the contents of what is here will have little effect on your future. These strategies deserve to be tasted, dived into, to surround you. Riding the delicious white waters of what is ahead will bring some adventures you will deeply prize and cherish. Who knows, the self you meet halfway may become your best friend.

I envy you the pleasure of what is ahead. Please accept our warmest, best wishes for this incredible journey in self-discovery. Let Socrates have the last word.

"The unexamined life is not worth living."

Sidney B. Simon

Introduction

> Vladimir: Say you are happy,
> even if it's not true.
> Estragon: What am I to say?
> Vladimir: Say I am happy.
> Estragon: I am happy.
> Vladimir: So am I.
> Estragon: So am I.
> Vladimir: We are happy.
> Estragon: We are happy. What do we do now,
> now that we are happy?

The two tramps in Samuel Beckett's play *Waiting for Godot* have come to dramatize "the theatre of the absurd." But their conversation also dramatizes the theatre of our everyday lives, where the absurd is often real, where we are all waiting, searching, looking for something.

Who am I? What do I want? Am I happy? (Or do I just think so because I repeat the words?)

Questions that defy answers?

More questions—the answers to which are often drowned out by the deafening roar of small-talk-humdrum that may be our daily life. Do I know what I value? Am I sure? Are my words and my actions consistent with my feelings and beliefs? What values do I hold that are especially important? Which ones am I truly proud to believe in, and which will I publicly affirm? Which would I be willing to die for?

Ultimately, it is our values that give us the stars by which we navigate ourselves through life. Yet how do we select them? How can we make any sense out of the clamoring and bewildering appeals running rampant in these baffling times? The "eternal verities" seem to be less than eternal; the familiar "shalt nots" so often don't relate to the complexities of our daily lives.

It was Thoreau who wrote, "The mass of men lead lives of quiet desperation." Ours is much too loud a world, transistorized beyond the point of finding silence, but the desperation is as obvious. It merely takes on a more frenetic tone as people try to find the values that give life meaning and direction. To clarify values, to find something to live by, may be one of the most significant thrusts a person can give to his or her life in this confusing and conflictful world.

The traditional pillars of education and religion have not adequately or contemporarily prepared us for choosing our personal set of values. In our everyday lives of decision-making, they have not taught us enough to help us adequately decide when an action is right and when it is wrong. They have not given us the necessary training and the skill to make conscious value decisions. Consequently, there is considerable confusion between right and wrong, between legality and morality; and a gaping discrepancy between what we say and what we do. We see this disparity in political life, in the lives of our cinematic heroes and heroines, and we see it right down the street in our friends and relatives and the lives they lead.

Everyone is <u>for</u> values. The problem is that they have become meaningless platitudes, or hypocritical meanderings.

This is particularly evident in the time-honored method for acquiring values, transference of values. We are <u>told</u> which are the right and good values. The assumption behind this kind of moralizing runs something like this. "My experience has taught me a certain set of values which I believe would be right for you. Therefore to save you the pain of arriving at these values on your own, and to avoid the risk of your choosing less than desirable values, I will effectively transfer my own values to you."

The major fault with this direct transference of values is that it results in, indeed often creates, the conflict between theory and practice. As T. S. Eliot states it in *The Hollow Men:*

> *Between the idea*
> *And the reality*
> *Between the motion*
> *And the act*
> *Falls the shadow.*

Lip service is paid to values, while our overt behavior often contradicts them. Thus we have religious people who love their neighbor on the Sabbath and spend the rest of the week jousting with him. And we have patriots who deny freedom of speech to any dissenters whose concept of patriotism is different from theirs. And we know only too well the disparity (campaign oratory) between what a politician promises and what he delivers. It is as evident in the gap between preaching and professing and the necessary doing.

Moralizing most often influences only people's words, and little else in their lives. Fortunately perhaps, this traditional approach is becoming increasingly less effective, because direct transference of values only works when there is complete consistency about what constitutes "desirable" values. But consider the situation today. We have one set of "shoulds" and "should nots" from our parents. The church often suggests a second. Our friends and "peer group others" offer a third view of values. And then, the chaos of value conflicts: views from opposing political groups; the dizzying kaleidoscope of tele-vision, advertising claims, popular magazines; militance of left or right; and the "counterculture." And . . .

So in the melee of contradictory claims, value transference has largely failed, and maybe it's just as well.

Bombarded by all these influences, we are ultimately left to make our own choices about whose advice or values to follow. Or to make no choice at all, and just drift.

But we have not learned a process for selecting the best and rejecting the worst elements contained in the various value systems that others urge on us. Too often the important choices in life are made on the basis of peer pressure, unthinking submission to authority, or the power of propaganda.

Another way of receiving values is by example, by way of the "exemplary life." This method sometimes bridges the gap between word and act, but still something is missing. How can we translate into our everyday lives the actions, however noble, of another person living a very different life?

Values simply don't transmit, and they cannot be taught; but they can be learned. If you accept that idea, you move away from moralizing and modeling. You move toward the more promising process of values clarification.

Values clarification involves a series of strategies that do not force one set of "right values" down everyone's throat. Nor down anyone's throat. Instead, values clarification tends to raise issues, to confront us with inconsistencies, to get us to sort out personal values in a unique way and at an appropriate pace. For example, play with this little values issue. If you are into baseball, which team do you hope will win the World Series? Which team do you hope will <u>not</u> win the World Series? Who is your "enemy team"? O.K., now a values clarification problem. Whom would you root for if every player on the team you "love" were to be traded for every player on the team you "hate"? Provocative little question, isn't it?

This kind of approach will help <u>you</u> look deeper into <u>yourself</u> to make judgments concerning prized values and to help sort out feelings, attitudes, and behavior, all those things that are merely value indicators.

If you are interested in theory, read on a bit more.

page xiii

If theory doesn't move you, skip right to the *How to Use This Book* section.

page xvi

And if you don't like to be told how to use a book, then jump right into the first strategy, *A Long Life and a Merry One.*

page 1

Do what you value. **Value what you do.**

Values clarification is a process which helps people arrive at an answer. It is not concerned with an ultimate set of values (that is for you to decide), but it does stress a method to help you determine the content and power of your own set of values. It is a self-audit, and an inventory of soul and spirit. A tool to help you freely decide between alternatives or among varied choices. It is a methodology to help you make a decision, to act, to determine what has meaning for you.

Values clarification is part of a much larger humanistic movement, one of a number of individually directed psychological and sociological theories that also embrace Re-evaluation Counseling and what has become known as Encounter or Interaction Groups. (They are all outgrowths of the Third Force in psychology, which developed from the Freud/Adler split much earlier in this century. The Third Force, as indeed one of its facets—values clarification, is much more concerned with the present and the future and less with exploring the past.)

What could the process of values clarification mean to you? Because it is directed to the present and the future, it is positive, personally affirming, individually focused, and success* oriented.

All values clarification strategies come from a basic definition of what a value—any value—is. Underpinning this book is the notion that nothing can be called a value unless it meets several rigorous standards.

These standards of valuing are based on the seven processes defined by Louis Raths, who was my teacher, a leader in the

---

*"Success" means much more than on-the-job success; it also means success in personal relations, or in enjoying a sunset, but its vocational implications are many.

xiii

progressive education movement and an admirer of the great educator John Dewey.

The processes center on three key words that are associated with values.

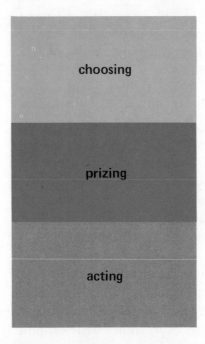

All values clarification strategies stem from these three words and from the seven processes evolving from choosing, prizing, and acting. Anything that does not meet all seven standards is not a value but a value-indicator. A value-indicator* does exactly what it says: it indicates that a value is in the process of "becoming."

---

* Value-indicators include goals or purposes; aspirations; attitudes; interests; feelings; beliefs and conviction; activities; and worries, problems, or obstacles.

Before something can be a <u>full value</u> it must meet these criteria. It must be:

1 chosen freely
2 chosen from among alternatives
3 chosen after due reflection
4 prized and cherished
5 publicly affirmed
6 acted upon
7 part of a pattern that is a repeated action

These are demanding standards. Many people have a multitude
of value-indicators but few values. Having value-indicators is
good, having values is better. When we realize the extent to which
values guide our lives—consciously or unconsciously—it's under-
standable that people with few values tend to be apathetic, conforming, inconsistent, and what psychologists often call ambiv-
alent (the simultaneous existence of conflicting emotions, such
as love and hate). The less we understand about values, the more
confused our lives are. The more we understand about values,
the more able we are to make satisfactory choices and take
appropriate action.

The person who has clarified his or her values will perform
zestful, independent, consistent, and decisive "acts of courage"—
not necessarily dramatic, much-publicized feats of heroism, but
rather acts based on the courage to say what has to be said and
to do what needs to be done.

It is a world we did not make, but one which we can yet shape
if we know how. This book is intended to help you begin the
task.

This book of adventures in self-discovery presents 31 strategies to help you locate, sort out, and build a set of values. The fact that there are 31 suggests that you might try one strategy each day for a month. This might be overly ambitious because some strategies are more complex or time-consuming than others.

The strategies are arranged in a sequential, bridge-building way. Each strategy stresses one or more of the seven values clarification standards, but you need not necessarily approach them in the order presented. Although the book is carefully structured, I would be inconsistent if I didn't allow for your choice and encourage your own spontaneous search.

Some strategies are designed primarily to help you take an inventory of a variety of aspects of your life; others are presented to help you make decisions, or to realize that in any value decision, "the piper must be paid," and to help you weigh any consequences that there may be.

These strategies are, in a real sense, "games." They do have rules, they are fun, and they do have an element of competition to them, a competing of the forces within you or friendly competition with others. But these are not "games that people play" merely to kill time. They are working tools of serious self-search, as thousands of teachers have discovered, who, having used them with students, found their own lives changing. Some of the strategies are thoughtful and complicated, others are more light-hearted. Try them alone or with friends. Some are so private that they apply only to you. Some you'll prefer to work on by yourself, others suggest that you share them with family and friends.

The shared strategies are group-oriented because only a consensus or group interaction will make them really meaningful. They encourage dialogue, and thus provide an opportunity to see the same questions from other viewpoints. Indeed, some of the strategies ask many questions and call for many answers.

Many of the questions are in their most simplified form, but they are simply (and directly) stated to cause you to take a position, to select an answer, and, hopefully, to act.

Some of the questions in the strategies may appear forced in themselves. For example, in the *Am I Someone Who . . . ?* strategy (page 23), questions 4 and 5 may seem arbitrary: "Am I someone who . . . would let my child drink?" and ". . . would let my child smoke pot?" The questions center around the word "let" (or permit). Unstated are a number of qualifying questions that come to mind, for example: "drink what, how much, when?" or "how old is the child?" etc.

Obviously, not all of these qualifiers could be included in these two questions, or in many questions throughout the book. Just try to make them apply as directly and simply to yourself as possible, and adopt them when that seems the thing to do.

The point is: these are general strategies and questions written to apply to as many people as possible. How they apply to you personally is for you to determine. Also, understand that certain questions require your imagination and your ability to project yourself into hypothetical situations.

Just as there's no right or wrong answer (although there should be an answer), so there is no right or wrong way of working through a question (although there has to be a question). For example, in another *Am I Someone Who . . . ?* question (number 1, page 23), you are asked whether you need to be alone. We understand that at some time everyone needs solitude, but it is my hope that you will answer the question as you understand it. As it applies to your needs.

Speaking of questions and answers implies a recording of answers to questions. And that "recording" is important. Throughout this book, you will be asked to commit yourself to writing, reminded to document your reactions to strategies, to write down answers.

31

questions

answers

xvii

To record responses requires a deeper kind of reflection than merely talking off the top of one's head. Even a quick look at the strategies will show that they all have a "you" component to them. They don't ask just for facts or information. They seek your "gut response" and probe your values about an issue. It will help you, the values clarifier, to put your answers in writing. This, in itself, helps clarify some important areas.

The clarification of values, especially as a written record, can help contribute to your sense of identity and self-worth. Values are vital in the search for answers to the question, "Who Am I?" Be willing to make that search, to know who you are, to commit yourself, to stand up and be counted. And only then will you have a set of values underpinning all that you do. You will know what is worth living for, and, if need be, what is worth dying for.

A long life and a merry one

What is worth dying for? Another way of putting it, what <u>was</u> worth living for? "If I were dead, who would mourn for me? What was the quality of my life? What did I accomplish?"

A rather grim <u>past-tense</u> way to begin a book dedicated to the present and the future. But it's also a thoughtful way. We all have choices as to how we will spend our future years. Hopefully, we will make the most of them. The intent of *A Long Life* is positive: the reality of death is not so important as the reality of life. How we live our <u>lives</u> is vital.

Take a piece of paper and draw a line across the face of it. Place dots at either end of the line. The dot at the left represents your birth date, write the actual date under it. The dot at the other end of the line signifies the date of your death. Over this dot write the number, your best guess, of the number of years you think you will live. Under this dot, write the estimated date of your death. (Let's hope you will want a long life and a useful one.)

Place a dot that represents where you are <u>now</u> on the line between your birth and your death. Then write today's date under this dot.

your birth

where you are now

This line is your Life Line. Does it represent a long life and a merry one? A good life? A worthwhile and a meaningful one?

To the left of today's date, above the line, write down a few simple words that represent what you believe are your accomplishments up to this point. To the right of today's date, indicate in a word or two, some things you would like to get done or experience before your death. Remember, many celebrated people "of accomplishment" have achieved little personally, for they have no repose within. Outer accomplishments count for only so much. "Accomplishment" here means making the most of yourself within yourself, within your personal capacity. Not surprisingly, it's a matter of values.

Look at this simple yet meaningful Life Line; study it and think about it. You may want to refer back to it to let it settle into your consciousness. How much time do you really have for a life of meaning?

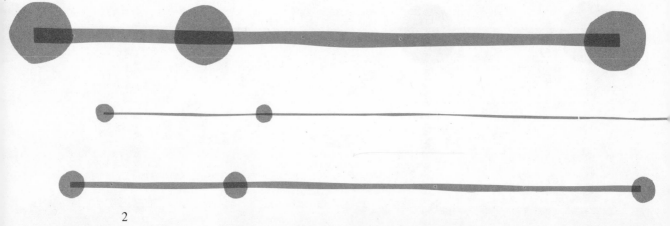

R.I.P.

Rest In Peace. Another somber reminder of "this mortal coil" can be found on gravestones and at the head of obituary columns. A reminder that life, however it is lived, ends with death.

Try not to view this strategy with <u>grim</u> subjectivity. Rather, with as much detachment as possible, try to view your death as you would objectively see your life. *R.I.P.* asks pointed questions about the quality of your life. From the vantage point of your inevitable death, this strategy encourages you to see your life more fully. It emphasizes liveliness: within the limits of your ability and the bounds of reality you can do whatever you want to do with your life. You really can, if you want it badly enough.

As you probably know, major news-gathering organizations have a staff of researchers and writers whose job it is to prepare in advance the obituary notices of celebrated persons. Their task is continually to update such information so that when "Senator John Filibuster Dies in Washington," or "Mary Smile, Hollywood Star Dies on Movie Set," the facts of their deaths and the information about their lives will be immediately available for the printing presses and the microphone.

Suppose you were a member of the "Obit. Staff" of a large metropolitan newspaper and were suddenly called upon to compose your own obituary notice. What would you say? Of course, part of your duty is to be as objective as possible. Here's the formula. It is a simple format.

Henry Jones, age ___ , died today from . . .
He is survived by . . .
At the time of his death, his principal endeavor was . . .
He will be honored for . . .
He will be remembered by . . . because . . .
He made contributions in the areas of . . .
He always hoped that he would . . .
The interment will be . . .
Flowers may be sent . . .
In lieu of flowers . . .

When you are finished, please give some thought to this obituary notice. You might want to ask some close friends to write their own obituaries and then compare notices: the facts, and the style of life behind those facts.

Here's a variation to consider. Take a piece of paper, draw a line down the middle. On the left side, write your obituary as it would appear in the daily newspaper if you were to die today. On the right side, write your obituary as you would like it to appear in the newspaper, if you were to die five years from today. Compare them. What could you do if you had (only) five more years to live?

Remember, you have charge of your life. R.I.P., but first L.W.V.—Live With Vitality!

4

Days of Delight

Let us assume, after having completed the last two strategies, that the reports of your death "are greatly exaggerated" and certainly premature. Now let's leap into the future, a future rich in fulfillment. The point of *Days of Delight* is to help you clarify what you want out of life. To do this, it is necessary to plan ahead.

Imagine yourself in the future, anytime from tomorrow to several years from now, and devise two *Days of Delight* that would be ideal for you. Imagine 48 hours of what would be the best possible use of that time for you. You can fantasize whatever you want within a 48-hour period.

Briefly write about your ideal two days, in your own words or in outline form, if you prefer. Try to detail all of your activities for the 48-hour period: what would you be doing, where would you be doing it, and with whom? Try to capture the complete flavor of the experience.

Your *Days of Delight* will probably reflect a very personal time. But if there are some aspects that you would like to share with others, ask a friend to write his or her two *Days of Delight* and compare your futures.

Remembering Auntie Mame's remark that "life is a banquet," this strategy could represent a kind of banquet with you fully enjoying the pleasures offered. Incidentally, Auntie Mame's complete comment was "Life is a banquet and most of the . . . (expletive deleted) . . . are starving to death."

For a later time: You may want to keep your *Days of Delight* essay as a reference guide to what you want out of life. And keep in mind the question, "How do I get it?"

The strategy *Discoveries* (pages 11-12) will help you sum up some important things about yourself as revealed in your *Days of Delight*.

A high score

Do you remember this scene from the Paddy Chayefsky film *Marty,* where Marty, the amiable but aimless Bronx butcher, is talking to his friend Ange about their plans for the evening?

"What do you want to do tonight, Marty?"

"I dunno, what do you want to do tonight, Ange?"

"I dunno, what do you want to do, Marty?"

Over and over, a treadmill to oblivion: indecision, a complete lack of interesting alternatives or choices. How many lives are this aimless, empty, colorless?

The person who clarifies his values generally knows what he wants to do and plans ahead for it. This strategy is one you will want to continue throughout life, in one form or another, preferably in the form of action. The important values-search question that underlies *A High Score* is, "What am I getting out of my life?"

You're not participating in a life of freely chosen values if you passively accept everything as inevitable. It is necessary to define and pursue your own goals. Otherwise you will not experience the feeling of self-action or self-satisfaction.

A High Score: Two Dozen Things I Love to Do will aid you in looking at those things that you most value and cherish. Then, when you know what these important foundations are, you can go about building the structure of your life more knowingly and alertly.

Take a sheet of paper and write the numbers 1 through 24 down the middle of the paper. To the left of the numbers, draw vertical lines that divide that part into seven columns.

things I love to do

Now think of things you most like to do. Big things or little things—it doesn't matter—as long as they are <u>important</u> to you. You might associate these 24 things with certain people, places, or seasons. Try to identify the situations, as they occur to you at random, by writing them to the right of the numbers you placed in the middle of the sheet. On the left side of the numbers, jot down certain information about the things you most like to do.

1 Put an M (for me) by those things you like to do alone. Put an O (for others) by the things you like to do with others. If you can go either way on a particular subject, put an M-O.

2 How much does this cost? Put a $ by any activity that costs more than $5.00.

3 Most of us change our preferences frequently. Put the letters N P (for not previously) by those situations that would not have been important to you a few years ago.

4 Some activities are spontaneous, others require planning. Put an S by those things that tend to be spontaneous and a P A by those you must plan ahead for.

5 Out of the 24 things you like to do most, what five are the <u>most important</u> to you? Number those five in order of your preference.

6 Reviewing each of the 24 items, try to remember when you last did it—jot down an actual or approximate date.

more

7 How often each year do you usually do each of these most favorite things? V O will mean very often, S will mean sometimes, and H E will mean hardly ever.

8 Put an X by those activities that you want someone you love to love doing.

9 Place the letter V by those activities that you know you have been validated for, that is, praised or admired for.

10 Put the number 52 by those activities that you would want to do at least once each week for the rest of your life.

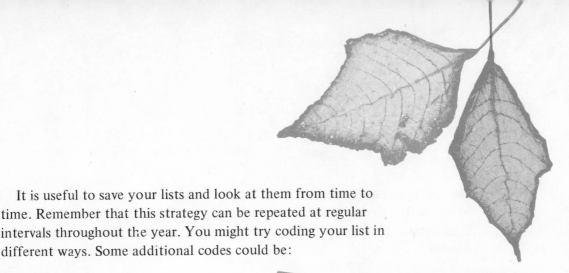

It is useful to save your lists and look at them from time to time. Remember that this strategy can be repeated at regular intervals throughout the year. You might try coding your list in different ways. Some additional codes could be:

1. We are often influenced by social convention. Put an I in front of those things you like that seem irregular.

2. Our society is still oriented to the work ethic. Frittering your time on nonproductive pursuits may be frowned upon. If any of your favorites are frittering (your time away), mark them F.

3. If any of the 24 relate to a particular time of year, mark them C L for calendar limitation.

4. Developing skill in any pursuit is a challenge. Indicate areas with D S wherever you want to improve yourself.

5. Exercise is essential for physical as well as mental health. An E can mark those activities that involve exercise.

6. Many families pass along traits and skills. Look for things you would like to pass along. Code these P A.

7. Some of your likes may involve the possibility of physical or psychological danger. Mark them C R for calculated risk.

8. Some activities help us grow intellectually and emotionally. Indicate S I for self-improvement.

9. Too often we don't spend the time we want to on things we like. Put an M O by these for more often.

10. Which of these activities are a source of relaxation? Mark those R.

more

11 The weather has a lot to do with your happiness. Show a W by these items affected by weather.

12 Sometimes enthusiasm for one of your activities can be so strong that you want to spread and share it with others. Mark these S.

13 Some of your favorite things (like smoking) might be a health hazard. Show an H H.

14 If you live to be 100 and are in good health, which of these activities do you think you will still enjoy? Write 100 by these.

15 Write the letters F Y next to those items that you think will not appear on your list five years from now.

16 Write the name of a person you most want to talk to about a specific item.

17 Next to each item, write the name of the person with whom, at what time, and under what circumstances you most like to engage in the chosen activity.

18 Next to each item, list five advantages, pleasures, gains, benefits, or satisfactions you get from that activity.

Look at your list as something that tells a great deal about you at this time in your life. Are you ready to draw some conclusions about yourself? Read the next strategy, *Discoveries*, and then ask yourself what you learned as you were going through *A High Score: Two Dozen Things I Love to Do.*

Discoveries

This may be one of the shortest strategies in this book. It also may be one of the most important. *Discoveries* represent great growth possibilities _if_ you are persistent and honest in your search for self.

    Discoveries is a private exercise _or_ a group strategy. It depends on _what_ you are discovering, whether the interaction of others is important. *Discoveries* _always_ follows other strategies. It complements and completes them.

Consider the following sentence beginnings:

I learned that I . . .
I was surprised that I . . .

I remembered . . .
I found it hard to believe . . .

I was saddened that I . . .
I enjoyed . . .

I never knew . . .
I plan to change . . .

    After a strategy like *A High Score: Two Dozen Things I Love to Do*, look at your coded data as a natural scientist might. What can you spot as trends, patterns, or threads? What does the data suggest? What have you learned about yourself? Notice the second pronoun, I, and how it is used in "discovery" sentences.

Discoveries can also be used in your everyday activities. For example, *Discoveries* could be made after a good party. Perhaps, "I discovered that I enjoy parties more when I take the risk of talking to people I don't know very well." *Discoveries* might be made about a relationship with others. "I learned that I need more recognition from my wife." Or it might be, "I discovered that I don't have enough stimulating people around me." *Discoveries* could also be made about your job, leisure-time activities, avocations, and enthusiasms. One of my students never goes to sleep without listing the *Discoveries* of his day. When you assume the responsibility for your own "valuing," and learn "I discovered that I . . . ," you will begin to enrich your search for values.

Data diary

"No person can know himself unless he is willing to reveal himself," suggests psychologist Sidney Jourard in his book *The Transparent Self.*

Many of us find that self-revelation, truthfully revealing ourselves and the realness of our lives, is a difficult thing. All too often we fall back on familiar reactions, what we <u>think</u> we know about ourselves. To really know, it is necessary to uncover basic things about our thoughts, habits, and actions. We can do this by finding out what gives shape to our life patterns; and then by our willingness to share at least some of that intimate knowledge—to give of ourselves. Otherwise we run the risk of not being whole people, but rather "hollow men, head pieces filled with straw."

The first step in knowing ourselves is to systematically collect information in a personal data bank. This has been, consistently, the raw material of values clarification. It necessarily involves the discipline of written record keeping. "Put it in writing" suggests permanence, a seriousness of purpose, a reservoir of things to look back on. These records needn't be formal. They can be written in your own style, comfortable and familiar, because you are your own record keeper. These documents are for your eyes only, unless at some future time you want to share them with others. There are two basic record forms: *Data Diaries* and *Reflections* (which is really a diary in reverse). Select one form, or better, use both—one in conjunction with the other, as a check on the past, present, <u>and</u> future.

A *Data Diary* should help you compile a great amount of information about yourself. It is not a general diary encompassing all of your daily activities. Rather, it is a specific kind of diary. Here are some of the *Data Diary* titles from which you might select.

1 Daily Diary
How do I spend my 24 hours?

2 Confidence Diary
Keep a barometer of your varying levels of confidence and insecurity. Explain causes.

3 Decisions Diary
Life goes on, and if it is to get better for you, only you can change it. Record what decisions you made and when you took action.

4 Conflicts Diary
Describe some of the circumstances surrounding any conflicts you were involved in or may have witnessed. E.g., What were the causes? How did you react? Was it resolved? If not, could it have been resolved?

5 Current Events Diary
What is new or particularly notable in politics or business?

6 Success Diary
List days you consider successful and some things that made your day.

7 Bad Day Diary
This is a record of the events on days when it would have been better to have stayed in bed.

8 Cash Flow Diary
How did income and outflow compare today?

9 Inspiration Diary
Record deep feelings, sense of God or higher reality, spiritual or religious experience.

10 Affirmation Diary
Record nice things done for you and said about you.

11 Depression Diary
List the things and people who may have dragged you down.

12 "I Gotta Be Me" Diary
Keep a record of where and
how your actions showed
your individuality.

13 Role Play Diary
Review your day in search of
the times and situations when
you were pretending, playing
a role rather than being
openly and honestly yourself.

14 Special Moments Diary
List the persons or situations
that evoked affectionate
feelings and thoughts because
they were pleasant, intimate,
and thoughtful.

15 "Go to Hell" Diary
Some people and situations
spawn anger and even hatred.
Keeping a record might reveal
a pattern.

16 I Learned Diary
Are you growing? This record
may give you a hint.

17 Don'ts Diary
None of us likes to repeat
mistakes. List people, places,
food, etc., that may be "no-
nos" for you.

After you have chosen one of the *Data Diary* topics, maintain
your specialized diary for at least two weeks. Then ask yourself
a number of organized, serious questions and write answers in
your diary. For example, in the *Disagreement Diary,* you might
ask yourself these questions.

1 How many times did I firmly
voice my disagreement? What
was the percentage of times I
did so?

2 In how many of the disagreements did I lose my temper?

3 What pattern emerges as my
way of handling disagreements?

4 In observing the ways that
other people handled their
disagreements, do I see a
pattern that I would find
worthy of emulating?

15

Or for the *Budget Diary* (*Cash Flow Diary*), you might ask these questions:

1 What purchases "bought" pleasure? disappointment?

2 What is the pattern of my expenditures? Do I spend more when I am by myself or with others?

3 How many purchases are free-choice expenditures?

4 What have I learned about my habit of spending money? How would I spend money differently?

Most important, after you have recorded your answers in your diary, write at least five *Discoveries* statements ("I discovered that I . . ."). This procedure is what leads to self-understanding.

After a midmonth review, start a new diary in a different data area; again keep it for two weeks, and then examine your raw data. You may want to keep *Data Diaries* as a continuing written record of the search for things that are motivating in your life. Hopefully, your *Data Diaries* will become increasingly meaningful. If we monitored our own lives with the intensity that we follow the stock market, the sports page, or soap operas, we would be witness to the most important drama of all.

Reflections

Whether you keep a *Data Diary* or not, but especially if you do, weekly *Reflections* can provide an organized but spontaneous and lively way of looking back over the week just lived. Just as the *Data Diary* is a singular personal way of recording your actions as they occur, so *Reflections* is a way of neatly seeing the week in review. Also, although it can be done privately, *Reflections* is a good values clarification strategy to do with others. It has the most serious of purposes, but it's fun and fun was created to be shared. Shared good spirits provide the most amiable of backdrops for self-revelation.

Reflections has four parts and all are directed to the present and future, yet it is based on data of the immediate past. The first part, *highpoints,* is especially meant to be shared with your family or friends.

Take a standard size piece of paper and fold it into quarters. In the first section or *highpoints* quarter, write down briefly where you were a week ago at this exact time. Then after some thoughtful consideration, list eight or nine *highpoints* of your entire week, i.e., those moments that gave you the greatest pleasure. Ask your group to do the same on their papers. Then star the two highest *highpoints* of the week. The group will require some reflective time. Please allow for it.

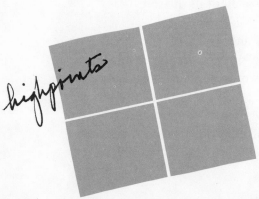

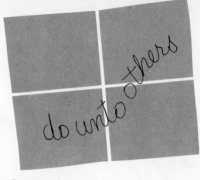

do unto others

What were three high moments within those two *highpoints?*
Jot them down. What were the nuances? If, for example, one of
the *highpoints* was meeting an old friend after a long absence,
what were the high moments within that meeting? If you do this
part of *Reflections* with a group, do allow for the lively exchange
of *highpoints* and the discussion it will generate. Then ask yourself and the others in your group, "What could I do to increase
the *highpoints* of my week?" In effect, the question asks, "Where
am I now, where do I want to be?" This question can be asked at
least six times. And then a private written note might be made
enumerating a minimum of six things that could be done to
increase the number of *highpoints* in your life.

Let's not forget that *Reflections* has three more quarters or
sections that constitute a full look at your present and future.
These three remaining quarters are the more personal *do unto
myself* sections. In the second quarter, note the names of people
who come to mind spontaneously in answering the question,
"Who was I in emphatic agreement with this week?" It is important to be aware of the people we agree with, and why we agree
with them. Who are they? Are they strictly people we depend on?
Are some of them people who depend on us? Our bosses, our so-
called superiors, or our friends, family, and those who look up to
us? Over a period of time, you will develop skills in determining
who they are. That is why *Reflections* in all of its quarters is a
notable enduring strategy.

With only so many hours in our day and week, it is important
to distinguish between the "nourishing" people and the "toxic"
people in our lives, to use Fritz Perl's words. We must ultimately
make this judgment, then do something to avoid those who draw
from us unfairly much more than they give. It is far more
productive to concentrate our time and efforts on those nourishing people who give as much as they take. This can be done. It

clearly takes guts to arrange people and values in a hierarchy of importance. But that's what values clarification is all about!

Reflections: there are still two sections to go. In the third quarter, ask yourself, "What plans did I make for the future this week? Answer by writing down these plans. Continually, week after week, keep this third quarter in mind. The cumulative effect may be staggering after a review of consecutive weeks.

Finally, in the fourth section of your *Reflections* page, list the ways that your week could have been better, "if . . . ." You will be interested to know that this part of the strategy is rare for values clarification. There are few "iffy" questions, so take advantage of the opportunity. Answer, "If I could have . . . ," how your week might have been better.

Reflections is a detailed strategy designed to help you discover yourself. If you question some of these time-demanding details, keep in mind that documented evidence is essential in promoting value thinking. In reviewing many weeks of *Reflections,* you may be surprised to note the absence of activities that are personally selected and satisfying. You may wonder just how many weeks have passed in this uneventful manner. You are not alone. Most of us walk a boring treadmill. But we don't have to. Take hold of your life, live it more creatively, enthusiastically, purposefully, and proudly.

Values journal

A *Values Journal* is a diary to share. It stresses two processes in the seven steps toward values clarification: prizing and cherishing your beliefs and behaviors, and publicly affirming them. It tends to point out what each of us values at the time of the entry in the *Values Journal.*

The format for a *Values Journal* is direct and quick. Write down some thoughts of importance to you at various intervals, perhaps once a day or twice a week. *Values Journal* entries are usually made for three months or more. Looking back, these entries will indicate something of the pattern and texture of your life and of your thinking over that period.

Contact a friend, selecting someone whose value-thoughts you are eager to hear. After two or perhaps three weeks, review and discuss with your friend all value-thoughts as they are clarified by these questions. Which of the *Values Journal* entries reflect your most cherished beliefs or attitudes? Which entries would you want to rewrite drastically at this moment?

Can you spot a pattern to the things you stand for, as they are revealed in your *Values Journal*? Select one entry in which you express a strong, positive opinion. Have you done anything about acting on that conviction?

In view of the *Values Journal* listings, try to make some summary statements about the following aspects of yourself and your life.

1. How do I, taking an average day as a spin-off, generally spend my time?

2. What are the things (at least five) that really interest me?

3. How do I view life as a whole? Is my outlook conditioned by influences outside myself?

4. What short-range and long-range goals can I honestly identify? What, ultimately, do I want to accomplish?

5. What are my primary commitments in life? (List in order of importance.)

6. What are some options that I reflect on, mull over, or enjoy imagining about?

7. Specifically, what five things do I most value about my life?

8. What conflicts or problems do I have about my life? Which ones did I personally create for myself and which ones are primarily caused by persons and situations outside my responsibility and control?

Oh, these are so easy to read over and then move on. But please go back. Select any two questions and stay with them for at least five minutes. I believe that enormous power and strength come from grappling with life. These questions try to illuminate your grapples.

am I someone who...?

We may think we know ourselves, but how well? How well do we really fathom the people close to us: husbands, wives, sweethearts, members of our family, our friends? Are we willing to probe and poke and dig to find out?

Learning about one's self is similar to an archeological dig. An archeologist finds a clue that leads him to suspect there's something interesting below the surface. He focuses his attention on a covered area and begins the unearthing process in his search for the treasure.

The initial digging removes large amounts of surface rocks and may be rough and crude. Yet as the archeologist feels the nearness of the desired objects, the uncovering process becomes one of carefully removing tiny trowels of dirt, gently brushing here and there, so as not to damage the anticipated treasure. This may be a long, continuing process, which is not easily abandoned because of the hoped-for reward. To gain precious knowledge about ourselves is something like that.

Am I Someone Who . . . ? is a friendly strategy. It's fun, but it is also earnest, intended to help you consider what you value, what you want out of life, what kind of person you want to become. It is also an "others" or group strategy. People like to answer questions that are personally directed to them. Throughout the country, in adult classes and seminars, this is one of the most popular adventures in values clarification. It is a simple, thoughtful exercise that can easily be repeated with new questions. After trying your hand, and your head, at answering the following questions, and after your family or friends answer them, make up a new list of 20 or 30 questions of your own. Not all questions need be serious. Some of them can be lighthearted, even whimsical. And they can appear in random order.

No special importance is assigned to any one question, and some of the questions may not directly apply to you. Also, remember that there are no right or wrong answers, just the

22

answers that you, and those to whom you give the questions, come up with.

   The directions are simple. Circle one of the codes. Y for Yes, N for No, and M for Maybe. Mark your choices in the book or, if others are to join in the strategy, on a piece of paper placed over the column. Watch the Maybes. Use them cautiously, please. One of the purposes of this strategy is to encourage definite stands. Try to avoid being an extreme middle-of-the-roader, what I call a compulsive moderate. Unless you feel Maybe quite strongly, answer all questions as they <u>might</u> apply to you, Yes or No. Here are 20 questions to begin with.

am I
someone
who

1 | needs to be alone? | Y N M

2 | watches television soap operas? | Y N M

3 | would kill in self-defense? | Y N M

4 | would let my child drink? | Y N M

5 | would let my child smoke pot? | Y N M

6 | is apt to judge someone by appearances? | Y N M

7 | can receive a gift easily? | Y N M

8 | is willing to participate in an encounter group? | Y N M

more

23

9 | eats when worried?   Y N M

10 | is afraid to be alone in the dark?   Y N M

11 | is afraid to be in a strange place?   Y N M

12 | could be part of a mercy killing?   Y N M

13 | could be satisfied without a college degree?   Y N M

14 | will order a new dish in a restaurant?   Y N M

15 | could accept sexual impotence or frigidity?   Y N M

16 | will publicly show affection to another person?   Y N M

17 | will put things off?   Y N M

18 | likes to stay up all night when friends visit?   Y N M

19 | is likely to have six or more children?   Y N M

20 | will probably never give up smoking?   Y N M

Now that you have answered these questions, you may want to give them to someone who knows you fairly well. Have that person do two things. First, code the answers. Then start over, this time guessing the answers that <u>you</u> made.

Now covering the answer column again, you might code the answers that you think that person made. The guessing and the revelation come full cycle. This strategy has almost endless possibilities, depending on how many people participate. After the group has answered and guessed each other's answers, sit down and talk about each other's messages, the messages we send, and how they are received by others. You can learn a good deal about yourself; about those participating in the strategy; about openness, congruency, and self-concept from sharing in this way.

Another variation is even more affirmative. Answer the questions preceded by the statement:

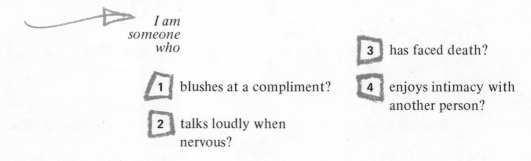

I am someone who

1 | blushes at a compliment?

2 | talks loudly when nervous?

3 | has faced death?

4 | enjoys intimacy with another person?

A concluding strategy after all questions have been answered is to revisit an old friend, the *Discovery* strategy. What did you discover, what did you learn about yourself? "I discovered . . ." is a continuing help. It aids clarity, reinforcing what you've found out. And it provides a good summary or windup for almost any other strategy. Keep it in mind.

Here are more *Am I Someone Who . . . ?* questions to use. To make it easier to refer to this section later, you might write Y, N, or M after each one of these questions.

am I someone who

1. will insist on traveling first class?

2. is capable of handling opinions different from my own?

3. enjoys leisure time for creative development?

4. experiences boredom and lacks motivation?

5. responds with compassion when others suffer misfortune?

6. likes to take over leadership responsibilities?

7. thinks interracial marriage is a good thing?

8. works diligently on every project undertaken?

9. will travel extensively during my lifetime?

10. reads the comics in the newspaper first?

11. has high ethical standards?

am I
someone
who

1 believes everything I read?

2 thinks that most politicians are dishonest?

3 thinks the Ku Klux Klan has its good points?

4 volunteers for jobs that are necessary but unpleasant?

5 would want to design and build my own home?

6 has an ambition to become a well-known author?

7 always looks up an unknown word in the dictionary?

8 enjoys working crossword puzzles?

9 frowns on gambling?

10 would marry for money and prestige?

11 needs to buy new clothes every season?

12 could get hooked on drugs or alcohol?

13 works for racial equality?

14 would die for my beliefs and values?

15 would rather eat out than eat at home?

16 considers a savings account very important?

17 is willing to pay a lot to have a good time?

18 needs several cocktails before dinner every night?

19 is easily swayed by the latest fads and gimmicks?

20 goes out and impulsively buys because I am easily influenced by ads on TV?

21 spends a great deal of time reading the latest best sellers?

more

12 would like to become a well-known sports athlete?

13 enjoys playing games rather than watching them on TV?

14 would compromise personal principles for a promotion and higher salary?

15 smokes three packs of cigarettes a day?

16 spends a lot of time worrying about things without doing something about them?

17 tries to do everything as perfectly as possible?

18 values friendship more than money?

19 would like a flashy sports car?

20 goes to as many X-rated movies as possible?

21 would like to be a famous movie or TV star?

section three

am I someone who

1 might seriously consider joining a radical, revolutionary-type organization?

2 would place a parent in a nursing home without considering other options?

3 often drives over the speed limit?

4 wouldn't drive without fastening my seat belt?

5 believes in the live-to-eat philosophy?

6 is concerned about corruption in business and politics?

7 would enjoy serving as a juror trying a criminal case?

8 likes to cook gourmet food?

9. finds it difficult
to praise someone for a
job well done?

10. likes to work with other
people rather than alone?

11. is conscientious about
saving fuel and energy?

12. yearns to become a very
successful business person?

13. gets an annual physical
checkup?

14. might cheat a little
on my federal income tax?

15. considers loyalty to a
friend or cause more
important than honesty?

16. keeps a daily journal
of events, reflections,
and experiences?

17. is able to take personal
risks without too much
anxiety?

18. considers failure a bad
thing?

19. tries to understand and
respect other opinions?

section four

am I someone who

1. likes conformity
rather than diversity?

2. respects the lessons
to be learned from a
study of history?

3. would like to be a
community organizer?

4. sets realistic life goals?

5. thinks being a street gang
leader is cool?

6. makes important decisions
without consulting others?

7. is inclined to blame
others when experiencing
failure?

8. sends greeting cards
for each and every
occasion?

9. carries on extensive
correspondence
with friends?

more

am I someone who

10 would rather fight than quit?

11 would enjoy owning a large sailboat?

12 is afraid of flying?

13 would like to hitchhike through Europe?

14 would not object to premarital sex for my children?

15 is usually late for appointments?

16 would donate my body to science research?

17 might rush into marriage?

18 falls in love right away?

19 has ever felt lonely, even in a crowd of people?

20 has a close friend of another race?

1 has had someone of another race home for dinner?

2 plans to vote for the same political party as my parents?

3 has had such bad problems that I wished I could die so I wouldn't have to face them?

4 thinks that women should stay home and be wives and mothers?

5 has been hurt by a friend?

6 thinks people should limit the size of their families to two children?

7 favors a law to limit families to two children?

8 would like to make some changes in my life?

9. thinks it is all right for older brothers and sisters to discipline younger ones?

10. would rather be older or younger than I am now?

11. would rather live someplace else?

12. knows someone who has fought in a war?

13. has ever seen a dead body?

14. would like to jump from a plane with a parachute?

15. thinks I will be only too happy to retire when the time comes?

16. would like to have different parents?

17. has seen someone die?

18. would like to take karate lessons?

am I someone who

1. would not want to be president of a company that produces napalm?

2. would like to have a secret lover?

3. would like my body to be cremated when I die?

4. could invite someone I couldn't stand to my home?

5. is fully satisfied with what I have accomplished in life so far?

6. thinks marijuana should be legalized?

7. would turn in someone for using drugs, if he/she were my friend?

more

8 has ever wanted
to really hurt someone
for something he/she
did to me?

9 has ever written a
"Dear John" letter?
Received one?

Just imagine how much you could learn about people in your life if you all took part in this strategy. I, personally, wish I had known this technique during those grim blind-date days. I might have sorted out so much faster who was worth really spending time with. It does, you will admit, go beyond who looks good in a bathing suit and who knows the most up-to-date dance.

There is even more to learn. There is you to learn. I hope you sense that deeply in the *Am I Someone Who . . . ?* strategy. And there is more to come. Read on.

What if...?

Let your mind wonder (<u>not</u> wander). Let it be free of the facts and statistics of the here and now. Let it fully partake of the <u>wondrous</u> and <u>wonderful</u>: the surprising, astonishing, and the admirable.

This strategy is similar to *Discoveries,* but it's different in that the purpose of *What If . . . ?* is speculative and does not depend on drawing conclusions from what <u>really</u> happened.

What If . . . ? is to be shared with others. Match your imagination with theirs. "Wonderments" can be a continuing *What If . . . ?* following many, if not all, of the strategies throughout this book. As mentioned elsewhere, this is one of but two "iffy" strategies that the process of values clarification permits. Values clarification is a process that doesn't allow for wishy-washy positions. It tends to help people toward being more definite and affirmative. At the same time, it does encourage healthy mind expansion and spontaneity.

So far, you have been asked mostly to answer questions and make statements. It is just as essential that <u>you</u> have a chance to <u>ask</u> questions. *What If . . . ?* is a simple and direct strategy that encourages probing, critical questions, and attitudes.

Upon conclusion of other strategies, such as *Days of Delight* or *Am I Someone Who . . . ?,* complete these sentences:

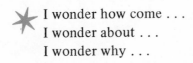 I wonder what would have happened if . . .
I wonder what would happen if . . .

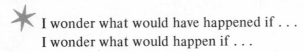 I wonder how come . . .
I wonder about . . .
I wonder why . . .

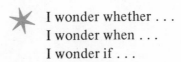 I wonder whether . . .
I wonder when . . .
I wonder if . . .

Here is a sample of real, live "I wonders . . ." given to me by one of my favorite teachers. Jane Stenger teaches at Apollo High School in Simi Valley, California. She has her students generate "I wonders . . ." all the time. And she does them, too, and shares hers with her students. Imagine how the family dinner table would change if people were given a chance to make "I wonders . . . ," and then to tell more about their feelings and thoughts behind their wonderings.

I wonder why I hate my new job
I wonder why I get depressed so easily
I wonder why living is so hard

I wonder why people get tired so easily
I wonder if I'll be on earth next Christmas
I wonder why it is so easy to lean on someone

I wonder what this world would be without love
I wonder why some people get so used to protection and security
I wonder what this world would be like without you

I wonder why some people can live without someone
I wonder why people get so lonely

I wonder why people spend so much time picking out each
other's faults
I wonder why people try to cover up their own faults by picking
apart someone else
I wonder why people can't pick out the good things instead

I wonder what I'll be doing three years from now
I wonder if I'll ever know what matters to me
I wonder if I'll ever find people like the people at Apollo

I wonder what other people are feeling
I wonder what I will be, because I'm constantly changing
I wonder why I'm scared of graduating

I wonder why people have to be alone when they love
each other so much
I wonder why friends hurt each other so much

I relearned that I need people
I learned that I am happiest when I am at Apollo
I learned that Apollo has transformed my life into humanness
and happiness
I relearned that Jane and her class have helped me grow the most
I've ever grown

values chart

One of the useful effects of values clarification is that the clarifying processes can be applied to the daily decisions that you
make. The end result of values clarification is to help you make
value decisions, whether they fall in the moral sphere or in your
everyday living, even to help you determine the products you
buy. Thus values clarification works on values over the whole
spectrum of life. All value decisions are threads that, woven together, form the fabric of your behavior.

It is of some importance to know why we buy this brand of
toothpaste or that brand of automobile. Or why we see a certain
movie. It's vital to know that we can make our own decisions,
rather than being conned or coerced into them.

The *Values Chart* will help you know whether your choices
are just value-indicators or full-fledged, high-flying, genuine
values conforming to all seven value processes.

To make your *Values Chart* is to make a permanent reference
and reminds us that most of our beliefs or actions rarely fit all
the value processes. This strategy indicates the steps that must
be taken to develop stronger and clearer values.

To make your *Values Chart*, take a piece of paper and, following the example of the illustration on page 38, divide it into two
sections. Label the first part Issues. On the second part of the
paper, write the numbers 1 through 7 across the top. These
columns represent the seven processes of values clarification.

Name some general issues you currently have feelings about,
such as corruption in politics or business, water and air pollution, population control, race relations, a specific election, a
community problem. Don't just use this list of issues, determine
the issues you are concerned about. Think of what affects you
personally and as a member of your community. List those
issues on the lines on the left-hand side of your *Values Chart.*
Next to each of these issues, write a few key words that sum-
marize your position or stand on that issue.

1 Was my decision made freely without external force or coercion?

2 Do I cherish the position that I have taken?

36

Now try to answer each question in the seven processes in relation to each issue. If you have a positive response to the first question, then put a check in the appropriate box. If you cannot answer the question affirmatively, leave the box blank. You are not being called on to defend the content of your beliefs. Rather this is an inventory of where you are at and what needs to be done if you are to make your stand a real value. The inventory helps you find out more about how you arrived at your convictions and how firm you are in them. Enjoy the process. Delight in the mysteries of how we all come to stand for what we do.

the seven processes

3

Did I do my homework, i.e., did I carefully evaluate the advantages and disadvantages of my decision and thoughtfully consider the <u>consequences</u> ?

4

Did I make my decision after examining all possible <u>options</u> ?

5

Have I practically <u>applied</u> and <u>acted</u> on my convictions and beliefs ?

6

Have I given <u>public</u> <u>affirmation</u> to what I believe ?

7

Does my behavior indicate that I act on these beliefs <u>repeatedly</u> and does it reveal a definite pattern and personal commitment ?

To what extent are these seven processes the basis for the values strategies you are doing? See if you can make a list of the seven processes from memory. Save your paper and look at it again at some future date. You will be able to see not only whether the content of your beliefs has undergone any change, but, more importantly, whether there have been any changes in the quality and degree of your convictions.

Some issues you may consider in the *Values Chart* might be expanded from the following questions.

Do you

1 have difficulty communicating with your parents/children?

2 think school environments affect the learning process?

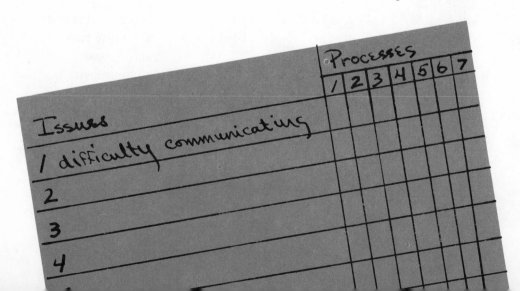

3 approve of sex education as part of a school curriculum?

4 contribute money to any political cause?

5 talk honestly and freely with your parents/children about sexual concerns?

6 think picking up hitch-hikers is a dangerous thing and should be avoided?

7 tend to be a health-food addict?

8 identify with and practice the religious beliefs of your parents?

9 believe that there is a serious erosion of moral standards in this country?

10 approve of mercy killing?

11 think that young people should learn to be competitive in school to prepare for the future?

12 frequently seek advice or counsel from older, more experienced people?

13 feel anxious and insecure about making personal decisions?

14 often wonder about your future and the future of our world?

15 have any problems about watching your weight?

16 support the goals of the Women's Liberation Movement?

17 think you will ever participate in a boycott of any kind?

18 believe that the income tax system is unjust?

more

Do you

1. feel that the news media (TV, newspapers, etc.) generally distorts the truth?

2. approve of a six month to a year trial marriage?

3. believe that today's young generation is more open and honest than the older generation is?

4. feel that self-discipline is better than imposed discipline?

5. like the idea of creating your own school curriculum rather than having school administrators do it?

6. frown upon people who resort frequently to four-letter words in their conversation?

7. think that physical punishment is sometimes a necessary disciplinary tactic?

8. feel free to discuss personal problems with your parents and friends?

9. value friendship above economic success?

10. have discriminating tastes in terms of the TV programs you watch?

11. think that violence on TV encourages violence in the street?

12. subscribe to a weekly news magazine and read it faithfully?

13. enjoy entertaining friends at your home?

14. like to eat at expensive restaurants?

15. worry about your financial security?

16. have rather high ambitions for your future?

17. enjoy spending time with your family?

Do you

1. feel that as a consumer you are being manipulated by big business?

2. have pleasant memories of your school experiences?

3. think the present grading system in schools is detrimental to the learning process?

4. like to be alone to think things out personally?

5. feel comfortable with silence?

6. think that labor unions are abusing their power to achieve selfish aims?

7. believe that busing schoolchildren will be a strong factor in bringing about integration?

8. feel strongly that the U.S. should continue to give financial aid to Third World countries?

9. believe that it is unjust to discriminate against homosexuals?

10. feel free to express your opinion with your boss or someone above you?

11. think most politicians are crooked?

12. make a conscious effort to really listen to another person?

13. have the ability to take personal criticism without feeling self-pity?

more

DO you

14 think you will ever become actively involved in a political campaign?

15 think gambling should be legalized?

16 ignore people who think differently from you?

17 think that you are prejudiced with regard to race, sex, nationality?

1 enjoy and appreciate listening to classical music?

2 want to own your own home someday?

3 feel satisfied with your present life style?

4 believe that human values can be learned but not taught?

5 approve of teen-age marriages?

6 feel optimistic about life and look forward to the future?

7 think you would take your children to religious services even if they didn't want to go?

8 think you would be upset if your daughter were living with a man who had no intention of marriage or your son living with a woman he had no intention of marrying?

9 enjoy smoking?

10 think you would raise your children differently from the way you were raised?

11 think you would encourage legal abortion for an unwed daughter or a son who had gotten a woman pregnant?

12 think you would change to a job you didn't really like because it offered $10,000 a year more than you now make?

I hope you catch some of the excitement that we in values clarification feel when we look at those random, sometimes highly emotionally charged opinions we have on the whole wide range of human experience. And then we realize that some of our ideas are clearly half-baked, because we haven't examined them very long and very hard. The *Values Chart* can show you which of your ideas need to go back into the oven, and what you need to do about some other ideas that are still just words and not yet actions.

Try hard to avoid doing a scene of self put-downs. I often tell our workshop participants, over and over again, "You are doing the best you can, for now! If you could do better right now, you would be doing it. Ah, but tomorrow, and the tomorrow after that. There's where the values clarifier does his or her richest and sweetest mellowing."

43

Priorities

*P*riorities is another dinner-table strategy. There are delightful possibilities for applying it socially to everyday decisions. It asks you and your family at the dinner table, or your friends across the lunch table, to rank choices and to defend those choices in friendly discussion.

This strategy dramatically illustrates the need to establish priorities. Knowing that this is a process—one of the seven processes—toward values clarification, you realize there are no right or wrong answers, but for each of us, there is a need to set up a priority of action.

In any decision, you have to be willing to take a values stand. This can be difficult, because you must accept the consequences of your action. Choices, some of them very attractive, must be eliminated. It's serious work.

But it can also be fun. *Priorities* probes your imagination and challenges your wit. Their application is "across the board," the bread board of the homemaker or even the board table of the busy administrator. The lessons of this adventure in values selection can heighten your personal life or your career.

Each day of your life you must make decisions between competing choices. Some of them are minor. "Shall I stay home tonight and watch TV or go to a friend's house for the evening?" "Shall I read a popular novel or a book that only I seem interested in?" And some are major decisions. "Should I buy a new car or make the present one last another year?" "Should I seek a new job, continue the present less-than-satisfactory one, or live on yogurt, sprouts, or welfare?" These are alternatives. Sometimes you have to decide among three or four choices, and establishing priorities then becomes increasingly difficult.

Many issues confronting us demand more time and thought than we give them. *Priorities* examines the whole area of making

choices and defending those choices in lively discussion. How
would you rank the following choices? How would your friends
rank them? In each case, don't just pick your first choice, but
state which is your second choice over the third choice.

1 Your parents are going to celebrate their twenty-fifth
wedding anniversary. What would you do for them?

☐ invite them to
dinner at a fancy res-
taurant and get tickets
for a movie or a show

☐ make plans to throw
a big party for them
and all of their friends

☐ give them an expen-
sive gift (something they
have always wanted)

2 You have only one parent and he or she is getting very old
and somewhat senile. You have your personal responsibilities toward your own family and spouse. What would you
do?

☐ make arrangements
to have your parent
transferred to a nursing
home nearby

☐ provide a small
apartment or some
other independent
living situation

☐ make provision in
your own home and
invite your parent to
share your living
arrangement

3 Your brother and sister-in-law are having serious marital
problems, problems which neither of them can resolve.
What would you like them to do?

☐ initiate legal action
for a divorce

☐ mutually agree to a
separation and take
responsibility for the
children on a rotating
basis

☐ in spite of the
estranged nature of
their relationship, stay
together for the good
of the children

*more
priorities*

4 Your birthday is coming up next week. What would you
   like your husband/wife to give you on this occasion?

   ☐ $15.00 to purchase
   your own gift

   ☐ a $15.00 present of
   his or her own selection

   ☐ a gift that was
   specially made by him
   or her for you

5 Your best friend has spent a great deal of time selecting a
   present for you. He or she personally gave it to you. You
   realize all this but really do not like the present. What
   would you do?

   ☐ take the present
   back to the store and
   establish credit for the
   future without telling
   your friend

   ☐ say thank you and
   keep the present with-
   out giving any indica-
   tion of your real
   feelings

   ☐ tell your friend that
   you appreciate his or her
   thoughtfulness, but
   that you honestly don't
   like it

6 You are scanning the job market for employment. Which
   of the following positions would you prefer?

   ☐ easy but physically
   exhausting and dirty
   work for a $300.00 a
   week salary, no chal-
   lenge involved

   ☐ difficult, long hours
   of dirty work for a
   $400.00 a week salary

   ☐ pleasant, simple work
   for a $200.00 a week
   salary

7 A close relative just surprised you by giving you a $50.00
   gift. What would you do with it?

   ☐ deposit it in your
   savings account
   immediately

   ☐ take a much desired
   trip

   ☐ throw a big party
   for your friends

8 You consider yourself a good, religious person. It is Sunday morning. What would you do that would most express your religious beliefs?

☐ play some of your classical, religious music on the record player

☐ go to church to hear a moving sermon by the minister

☐ prepare for a big noon brunch for the whole family

9 The population problem is very serious and involves every country on this planet. What steps would you encourage to help resolve the problem?

☐ volunteer to organize birth-control information centers throughout the country

☐ join a pro-abortion lobbying group

☐ encourage the limitation of two children per family and have the parents sterilized to prevent future births

10 Pretend that for half a year you have been a guest with a family that has very strong religious beliefs. They go to church every Sunday morning without fail. Their religious affiliation is different from yours. Which would you do?

☐ go with them to their church service

☐ go to a church of your religious affiliation

☐ stay at home and not go to church

11 Imagine that you are all alone on an island in the South Pacific. Which would you want to have along?

☐ the Encyclopaedia Britannica

☐ the Holy Bible

☐ the writings of William Shakespeare

more
priorities

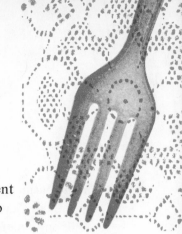

12 Most of us find it difficult to accept the death of a parent or a close friend. Which would you find most painful to accept?

☐ the death of your father or mother ☐ the death of your husband or wife ☐ the death of your closest friend

13 If you were just informed that you were to receive a large inheritance, how do you think you would spend it?

☐ on various educational endeavors ☐ take a first-class trip around the world ☐ on personal preferences and the entertainment circuit

14 If you had to make a choice, which of the following would you most not want to be?

☐ paraplegic ☐ deaf and mute ☐ blind

15 Which of the following categories would you not want to associate with?

☐ shoplifters ☐ drug pushers ☐ confidence men

16 What would you feel most capable of doing?

☐ being a community organizer in an urban inner-city neighborhood ☐ spending at least two years in the U.S. Peace Corps ☐ donating 5 percent of your income to charitable causes

17 What group of people carries the greatest stigma in today's society?

☐ junkies ☐ unwed mothers ☐ interracial married couples

18 How would you characterize your handling of money?

☐ easy come-easy go ☐ buying only at end-of-season sales ☐ miser

19 Your husband or wife is a very attractive person. Your best friend is very attracted to him or her. How would you want them to behave?

☐ maintain a clandestine relationship so you wouldn't know about it ☐ be honest and accept the reality of the relationship ☐ proceed with a divorce

20 What personal qualities would you like your best friend to have?

☐ ability to listen with compassion and understanding to your problems ☐ always tell you what you want to hear ☐ tells you the truth no matter how much it hurts

21 Someone close to you has just written a novel. You don't like it. Your opinion about the book is asked for. What would you do?

☐ say that you like it (because you don't want to hurt his feelings) ☐ be honest and say what you really think ☐ take a middle course and give it faint praise

*more
priorities*

22 What qualities in a husband or wife would be most annoying
to you?

☐ not caring about
keeping things cleaned
up

☐ always interrupting
you when you are
trying to talk

☐ being careless about
keeping the books
straight and spending
too much money

23 If you want to terminate a relationship with someone you
have been dating steadily for the last two years, how would
you go about doing it?

☐ write a "Dear John"
letter

☐ do it in a face-to-
face situation

☐ break it off through
a telephone call

24 Which job would you find most exciting and interesting?

☐ school teacher in an
inner-city urban school

☐ working with
mentally retarded
children

☐ social-action coordi-
nator for a progressive,
affluent suburban
church

25 When you were a student in the early elementary grades,
which did you like least?

☐ weekly show-and-
tell time

☐ recess/playground
activities

☐ reading aloud to the
class

26 If you had to give up one of the following, which one
would be the easiest to relinquish?

☐ freedom to partici-
pate actively in the
democratic process

☐ freedom to accumu-
late wealth and
personal property

☐ freedom to worship
as you want

27 Which one of the following issues poses the greatest threat
to the future of our planet?

☐ pollution of our air   ☐ crime and violence   ☐ poverty, famine, and
and water   overpopulation

28 If you were on a university campus and a riot broke out,
what would you most likely do?

☐ join the protesting   ☐ run to your dorm   ☐ observe the action
mob immediately   and lock yourself in   from a safe distance
                          your room

29 If you were a parent, what would be the most horrendous
news you could hear about your son or daughter? Would
the sex of the child make any difference in your order of
priorities?

☐ that he/she is   ☐ that he/she is a   ☐ that he/she plans to
sexually promiscuous   kleptomaniac   drop out of school

30 As you grow toward middle age and older, what physical or
medical concerns will you worry about?

☐ cancer   ☐ heart attack   ☐ gradual loss of vision

31 In what Federal Funding Program areas would you prefer
to have cutbacks made?

☐ defense budget   ☐ educational   ☐ economic aid to
                          programs and research   foreign countries

32 Which would you rather be?

☐ a black American   ☐ a black African   ☐ a black European

51

33 Which is most important in a friendship?

☐ loyalty ☐ generosity ☐ honesty

34 Where would you rather live?

☐ on a farm ☐ in the suburbs ☐ in an inner city

35 Which would you rather be?

☐ an only child ☐ the youngest child ☐ the oldest child

36 Which would you least like to be?

☐ very poor ☐ very sickly ☐ disfigured

37 Which do you think more money should be spent on?

☐ moon shots ☐ slum clearance ☐ cure for cancer

38 Which would you rather have happen to you if you had bad breath?

☐ be told directly ☐ receive an anonymous note ☐ not be told

39 Which would you most like to improve?

☐ your looks ☐ the way you use your time ☐ your social life

40 If you had $5000 to spend on decorating a room, would you spend

☐ $2000 for an original painting, the rest on furniture? ☐ $4000 on furniture and $1000 for an original painting? ☐ the entire sum on furniture?

41 What is the most serious problem in your community today?

☐ discrimination in jobs and housing   ☐ transportation   ☐ hunger

42 Which would you most like to be?

☐ owner of a small business   ☐ employee in a large corporation   ☐ employee in a small business

The list of *Priorities* to rank order is absolutely endless. These *Priorities* run the whole gamut of human existence—from money to sex back to child rearing and into politics, religion, death, and race.

This kind of rank ordering becomes one of the most useful values clarification skills in a person's life. Once you begin to do enough of it, you start to use it on the real problems that encircle your real life. You do it in a restaurant when you choose from the menu. You do it when you have to pick the place to go for summer vacation. You do it when you realize that you can only have four couples to dinner, and you decide who the four will be.

Each of you who is a parent could leave your own children no legacy more precious than for them to have years of experience in knowing what they want, having learned to set their priorities and rank order the marvelous items in life's cafeteria.

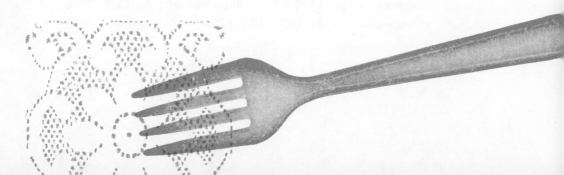

A matter of pride

"Pride goeth before destruction, and a haughty spirit before a fall." The biblical injunction to avoid self-puffery is a valuable one. But unreasonable and unbridled pride is not what we are speaking of here.

Let the following situation define the right kind of pride. A family is sitting around the dinner table. As various courses are served, and interspersed with other conversations, each member of the family is asked to complete the sentence stem, "I am proud that . . . ." Perhaps that person will say, "I am proud that we all love each other," or "I am proud that we can all be together to share this meal," or "I am proud that we care about each other more than we care about material possessions," or "I am proud that my sisters and brothers are willing to share their problems with me." Sometimes responses can be directed to a given category, for example, ecology, fighting racism, or sexism.

In this example of community or familial sharing, pride becomes part of a self-affirming ritual, almost a dinner-table blessing. This is the kind of pride, of self-esteem, that this strategy encourages.

A Matter of Pride is a group activity. It can become an important part of your daily affirmation. Perhaps a family dinner-table activity as described above.

You can't have a decent self-concept of who you are as a whole person without pride. Cherishing and prizing self is one of the criteria in defining self-values. False humility is as harmful as false pride. Be proud of what you do and what you are. Be willing to publicly affirm it. Regard your pride as a present to be shared.

A Matter of Pride will encourage you to do more things from which you can take pride. Think about what you have to be proud of in relation to some specific area or issue. It might be conservation or ecology, politics, social action, everyday activities, perhaps a demonstration of generosity of spirit or kindness.

People cannot be expected to be proud of everything they do or feel. But you should be able to define those things about which you feel good. Here is *A Matter of Pride* checklist.

things I am proud of

* Something that I recently made as a gift for someone special

* My ability to organize my work

* Some aspects of my last year's vacation

* My response to the energy crisis

* My savings account

* My family

* What I can accomplish independently of others

more

things I am proud of

* My many good and loyal friendships

* My difficult decision within the last year that required taking a risk

* A sports accomplishment

* The way I responded to a friend who was in need

* My nationality and family customs

* Something I did that did not require a great deal of courage but is a source of satisfaction

* Something unseemly that I was very tempted to do but did not do

* Praise I received for some special achievement

* My ability to express my opinions, even when they differ from others'

* My responsibility for making someone else very happy

* My good taste in clothes and talent for dressing well

* Some difficult skill that I learned recently

* I realized a long-sought-for goal

* Helping someone through a difficult problem

* Something I did to help the pollution problem

* Something I did that expressed my honesty and moral principles

* A time when I asserted real leadership

* My driving record

* Self-discipline regarding my eating and drinking habits

* I showed extreme sensitivity to someone else's feelings

* I helped someone in financial trouble

* I helped a parent and child get together again

* I did something about racial and sexual equality

* My willingness to participate in the democratic process

* The religious beliefs that I live by

* I helped an elderly or sick person

* A response by me that involved danger and required physical and moral courage

* An inherent talent I have and use successfully very often

* Time when I was especially creative

* It was difficult to forgive a friend but I did it

* An occasion when I was particularly open and honest

* It was difficult to tell the truth but I did it regardless

* I helped a younger brother or sister understand a problem

* A surprise I planned for someone dear

* My ability to think positively about people and the world

* Something I did that demonstrates my love for nature and beauty

more

things I am proud of

* An occasion when my good example inspired others to follow

* Something I learned recently that helped change my perspective

* My discriminating tastes regarding movies or TV

* A conversation where I listened carefully and became involved in what someone else was trying to say

* Something I read recently that required much thought

* An accomplishment that was difficult and challenging

* Attention to my family that showed my concern

We see so many people on the streets who clearly do not have pride. They are the people who seem to slink by, who avoid your eyes, who convey just by their curved bodies that they don't feel a sense of pride and worth deep within themselves. Each of us needs to stand tall and to be able to receive warm validation from our families and our peers for those things we can be justifiably proud of. A family that gives us opportunities to tell each other what we are proud of could do wonders to make us radiate the fact that we like ourselves. It is, indeed, a matter of pride.

Interacting opposites

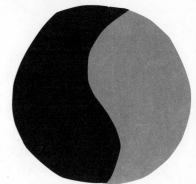

There are many contrasting Yins and Yangs in our life. The Oriental life symbol that represents these *Interacting Opposites* has been interpreted in a variety of ways, but always as illustrating opposition-in-unison, the seemingly contradictory but actually complementary forces that together combine to offer challenge and sometimes conflict in our lives. There are always opposing directions, elements, and ideas that we have to cope with: the notions of self and others; duty and pleasure; obligation and freedom.

Things diametrically opposed often complement each other. As F. Scott Fitzgerald observed in *The Last Tycoon:* "The true test of a good and fair mind is its ability to hold two opposite ideas at the same time, and still function." Values clarification helps us balance these dualities and also to make decisions.

The process of clarifying our values and giving meaning to our lives is a deeply rational one, never whimsical. It is in the most significant sense an intellectual process, yet values clarification recognizes, as the ancient Greeks did, that the "Dionysian" element of emotion or creative "irrationality" is as important as the "Apollonian," the clearly defined and well-organized element. Values clarification stresses that the life of feeling is as important as the life of the mind. Both are equal parts in our Yin/Yang existence.

Values clarification emphasizes spontaneous vitality as well as planning ahead; the joy of life as well as the discipline of self-decision.

Interacting Opposites is a special kind of inventory, an inventory of complementary opposites. It is a personal kind of exercise that challenges you to make rational judgments that are often based on feelings.

Interacting Opposites: divide a sheet of paper into four quarters. In the first section or left quarter, list ten people you like to be with, friends with whom you enjoy spending time. In the right quarter, list ten places you like to go, places in which you are happy to be, your favorite places. In the lower left-hand section, list ten people with whom you don't like to spend time. In the lower right-hand quarter, list ten places that tend to make you unhappy, places where you don't like to spend much time. What you then have is some information on opposites.

With the data elicited from *Interacting Opposites,* ask yourself the following questions.

What would happen if you took the ten people you like to be with, one at a time, to the ten places in which you don't like to spend time?

If you took the people you don't like to spend time with to the places you like, would it ruin those places?

What changes would you have to make in the places you don't like, to make them places you do like? Is that possible?

How often have you taken the people you like to be with to the places you like to be in?

What should be done for the people in the lower left-hand quarter of your *Interacting Opposites* page if you wanted to raise them to the upper left-hand section?

Finally and very significantly, what *Discoveries* can you make from this experience? What more do you know now about yourself, other people and places? And did you keep it playful while you were discovering?

I want values clarification to be one of the desserts at the banquet of life. I want the search to be serious and disciplined, but I also want all of us to throw our heads back and bellow at some of the absurdity of this marvelous thing called living.

Who comes to my house?

This is a question that only you can answer and only you can act on. It's a factual question involving real people and real expenditures of time. But it is also an inventory of the symbolic warehouse of your life. Perhaps now is the occasion to examine the stock on your shelves and set your store in order. Try to keep a balance between the necessity of planning ahead and the joy of spontaneity. Both are important in doing this kind of stock taking. Just as in any inventory, it's important to do this on paper for permanence of record and as a spur to action.

Do you recall the second section of the *Reflections* strategy, *Who was I in emphatic agreement with?* That is a question that has relevance to this inventory. How many disagreeing and disagreeable people do you feel you just <u>have</u> to put up with? Everyday bores on the job or in casual meetings? People you don't want to spend time with, especially at home, in your sphere of privacy? How many freeloaders come to break bread with you but offer very little in return? How many people are invited to your house only because you feel obligated to them?

When you come to think of it, there is something silly, certainly something nonessential, about paying off obligations, about spending too much precious leisure time with people who are millstones. The aim of this strategy is not only to determine who comes to your house, but what kind of people they are, whether they share themselves and enrich your life. Be honest (of course) and chart your own values.

Because mealtime, the act of breaking bread, is traditionally <u>the</u> act of hospitality, consider who has come to your house for a meal over the past year. Take a piece of paper, divide it in two. On one side list those people, either by name or initials, who have come to your house to share food. On the other side of the paper, list those people whose house you have gone to for a meal during the past year. Next code all names R, F, or O for Relative, Friend, or Other. If they fall into two categories, such as R and F, then designate them by their primary relationship, their meaning to you. After you have coded the names, star those who are special, very special: those people who give you great pleasure, who nourish your life by coming to your house, or who offer you much at their houses. On both sides, mark an X next to the names of those people who are dispensable, that is, if they stopped coming, it wouldn't be a loss.

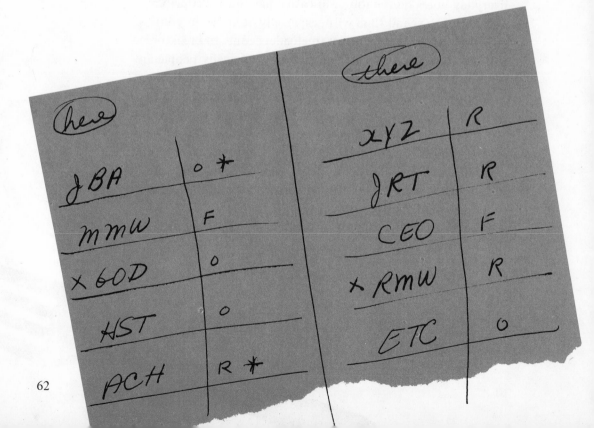

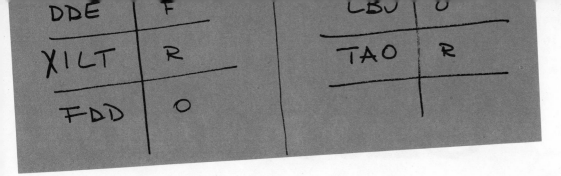

How many people fall under the category of burdens, either as relatives or business associates or unsharing friends? Think of the time that all of these people absorb in the course of the year.

There are, of course, "Responsibility People," those toward whom we have an important personal obligation, perhaps an elderly relative or infirm "other." These are responsibilities that, for the most part, we bear graciously, keeping in mind the inevitability of the aging process. To be kind and to help those who need us demonstrates a personal value we respect.

On the other hand, we can choose to spend our time, as much as possible, with those who give as they take, who offer at least as much as they receive. Keep in mind that while it is not necessary to agree emphatically on every issue with these "sharers," there might be a value basis for agreement with those people you elect freely to spend time with.

As you assess your relationships, it is important to do something about your discoveries. To be closer to those who mean very much to us, let them know how significant they are. Perhaps there is an occasion to celebrate, let them know by letter. But the best way to let people know of our caring is not just verbal or only words on paper, it is by our actions, continuing, meaningful acts of affection.

As a result of this inventory, perhaps fewer people will come to your house, but those who do are likely to be a part of the joyous celebration of life. Friends upon friends.

Slice of life

Slice of Life is an inventory strategy to help determine how
you spend your life, how you slice it into expenditures of time,
energy, and money. This background information is important
if you want to increase your joie de vivre. The *Slice of Life*
strategy can also be used to raise some thought-provoking
questions about the ultimate purposes of life. Keep in mind that
values are defined by action and by a consistent <u>pattern</u> of
action. What you say is not as important as what you do.

 Slice of Life is direct and dramatic. Draw a large circle or pie
on a piece of paper. This represents a certain area of your lifetime expenditures, how you use a typical day. Divide your circle
or pie into four quarters using dotted lines. Each slice represents
six hours. Now estimate at the bottom of the piece of paper
how many hours or parts of an hour you spend on each of the
following activities during a typical work day.

 How many hours do you spend
1 sleeping?
2 at work on-the-job?
3 at work that you take home?
4 with friends, away from your place of work?
5 alone, pursuing a hobby, reading, or watching TV?
6 on chores around the house?
7 with family, including mealtime?
8 on miscellaneous activities?

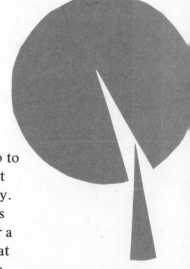

 Your approximations of time expenditures should add up to
24 hours. Now divide the slices of your time-pie to represent
the segments of the 24 hours that you spend on each activity.

 After completing your first pie and seeing how your life is
sliced for 24 hours, you might want to project a week pie or a
month pie to see graphically how your time is spent over that
period. Or you might make a work pie and see how your life

on-the-job is spent. For example, a work pie can be drawn to show the slices that are creative, interesting, dull but important, and busy work (dull and relatively unimportant).

There are many other areas that can be looked at as slices of the pie of your life. Further examples are: a pie with slices to represent where your money goes each week; a pie of the kind of books, magazines, and newspapers that you read or TV programs that you watch; a pie that represents a subjective inventory of your life, on which you can slice the proportions of the day that you feel high, neutral, or low.

Of course, there is no right way to slice your pie of life. Each of us lives a different life. You may not be inclined to change the particular ingredients in your pie. The emphasis here is on inventorying and looking at your life more closely.

After completing each pie of life, you might ask yourself these questions.

1 Would you like to change the various sizes of your slices?
2 If so, draw a "perfect" pie of your life. How large do you want each activity-slice to be?
3 What might you actually do to change the size of your various activity-slices?

You might record the answers to these questions in your *Values Journal* for future reflection.

The next time you are with some friends, get them to do some pies, too. I promise the flurry of "I discovered that I . . ." sentences will beat the excitement of almost any parlor game you can play.

65

Take shelter!

Take Shelter! may seem like an unusual imperative to come upon in a book devoted to openness and the open-awareness of self. But it is not at all unusual, as you will see. *Take Shelter!* requires that you open your mind to others' values and make tough choices.

This strategy is a group activity and can be a very lively game. It is a problem-solving exercise that asks you and your friends to make choices from a host of judgments and value issues. Values differ and it is often difficult to know objectively the "best" values. *Take Shelter!* demonstrates that we need great patience and sensitivity when listening to people whose beliefs differ from our own.

Gather six or seven friends into a group and then take shelter! This is the situation.

Your group is responsible for the welfare of Human Ecology Communes throughout the world. These communes bring together a variety of different kinds of people from all areas of life to see if humans of widely differing backgrounds and outlooks can live together peaceably and productively. Suddenly you learn that the "life balance" at one of these communes is dangerously upset because of unauthorized nuclear experimentation. The lives of all commune members are imperiled by radioactivity. You receive a desperate call from the leader of that commune asking for help. There are ten people at the commune, but enough water, food, air, and space in their anti-radiation shelter for only <u>six</u> of the people for three months, the length of time they will have to spend in the shelter.

They know that, should they decide among themselves which six are to go into the shelter, they are likely to become irrational, even violent. That is why they are calling you to determine which six are to be saved. They will abide by your decision.

Your group at Human Ecology Headquarters has only 30 minutes to make its decision. If you do not, all members of the commune will perish from radioactivity. The six who are selected for survival must be in their shelter in half an hour.

The question before your group is one of human life and of human values. Your choice is very important. You cannot let the ten people fight for survival among themselves, and you must hurry in your decision.

This is all you know about the ten people:

1 nuclear scientist;
age 47;
his careless experiments
caused the dangerous
radioactivity

2 his wife;
four months pregnant

3 Marxist revolutionary;
third-year medical student

4 famous psychologist-author;
60 years old

5 television celebrity;
host of innumerable
talk shows

6 brilliant female statistician;
25 years old

7 alcoholic priest;
50 years old

8 professional football player;
very low IQ

9 high-school sophomore
and majorette

10 former presidential assistant;
disbarred lawyer;
clever but shifty

That's the strategy. You and your group have 30 minutes to determine which six should go into the shelter. Someone in the group should give 15-, 10-, 5-, and 1-minute warnings.

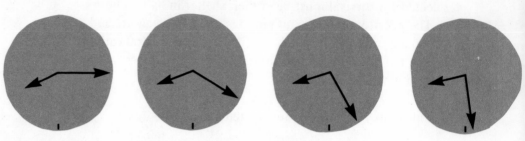

After your group has made its selections and has argued the reasons why, there are a number of basic questions that should be discussed. Ask your group to try to disregard the content of the *Take Shelter!* strategy and to examine the processes by which decisions were made and the value implications. It's best if one of the group is chosen to be a discussion leader.

These are the questions.

1 Did you listen to the opinions of others in your group?

2 Were you inclined to change your mind because of group pressures? Or, if you did change your mind, was it because of logical and persuasive arguments?

3 Did your single-mindedness prevent your group from reaching a decision in time? Did someone else's?

4 After your group arrived at a decision different from yours, did you still feel you were right?

5 What do your selections tell you about your values?

Sometimes these questions about the processes and the value implications of *Take Shelter!* are as exciting as the game itself. Certainly they are the important part. Why not write down some of these conclusions in your *Values Journal*, or later refer to the *Discoveries* strategy and ask yourself, "What did I discover about myself after playing this game with friends?" You may learn something new about yourself each time a new group competes. You may also learn something about the <u>kind</u> of friends you have.

Take Shelter! can be played in many ways. Here are a number of variations:

1. The descriptions of the ten people can be varied to suggest other values. For example, the shelter group could include:

a the same nuclear scientist responsible for the radioactive peril.

b a skilled manual worker; 40 years old; illiterate.

c a policeman with a gun; strong law-and-order man suspended from the police force for brutality.

d a blind Orthodox rabbi; 70 years old.

e a young female physician; capable but known to be unstable.

f a 46-year-old jazz musician; former narcotics addict and pusher trying to go straight.

g a 22-year-old female-rights militant; no special skills.

h an architect; homosexual.

i a 26-year-old painter and jack-of-all-trades.

j the painter's 25-year-old wife; spent the last nine months in a mental hospital; still under heavy sedation. They refuse to be separated.

2 Instead of determining which <u>six</u> people should go to the shelter, suppose your group were to select only three or two? Who would they be?

3 Before making any selection, ask your group to rank the ten candidates in order of desirability. What qualities would prevail?

4 Rather than discussing which of the ten should go to the shelter, either have each member of your group privately draw up his or her own list of six candidates for survival or rank all ten in order of desirability. Then after the lists have been privately drawn, the open discussion would begin.

5 Finally, how would each of you persuade each of us that <u>you</u> should be one of the six?

This strategy
was suggested by Joe Levine,
a former colleague of mine
at Temple University.

Wonder workers

Wonder Workers is another challenging group strategy-game to play with your friends or with your family, especially when there are children present. Kids of grammar-school age, indeed of all ages, love this game. Once again, don't overlook the fact that values clarification and the search for self-knowledge should also be a spirit-quickening and lighthearted endeavor. The end is serious, but the means, many of the strategies, need not be solemn.

Wonder Workers poses an interesting values clarification problem, one that often arises when you are confronted with many attractive choices. It is designed to help you get in touch with your feelings about what is important to you. The strategy also increases your awareness of what you want to become.

Here are the Wonder Workers—a group of 14 experts in their fields. They have agreed to offer you their exceptional services, services that are known to be 100 percent effective. Which of these Wonder Workers can best give you what you want?

Choose the five Wonder Workers you value the highest; that is, the five whose gifts you would most like to receive. Then pick five more names. This leaves the remaining four Wonder Workers in the least desirable group. Think about your choices.

Here are the Wonder Workers.

wonder worker **1**

Phree N. Eesie
His expertise is authority. This person will guarantee that authority figures will never intimidate you again. Here is an expert who knows all the secrets of control and subtle manipulation. The professional services offered will give you instant immunity from all authority that you feel is unjust (school administrators, police, your boss, politicians, and government, even the military forces!).

wonder worker 2

Gerry Atricks

This person will assure you of a long and active life (as many years as you want). Dr. Atricks knows how to slow down the process of growing old. You won't know illness or the loss of any of your functions.

wonder worker 3

Professor Momenpop

This person's expertise lies in the area of parent-child relationships. She maintains that with her counsel, all the problems you have with your parents—past, present, and future—will be solved almost instantly. Your parents will admire your every habit and will be a strong supportive element as long as they live. (You can say good-bye to the generation gap!)

wonder worker 4

Dr. Will I. Skinner

This internationally renowned plastic surgeon has the technical skills to transform your physical appearance to whatever you want with no pain whatsoever. He can even change your body structure and size through his unique application of hormones. All that you fantasized as ideal physical appearance will become a reality for you.

wonder worker 5

Mr. U. R. Sette

He is an expert in the field of vocational guidance, college and job placement. A choice of college or job position is yours to make. Opportunity and success are guaranteed. The location can be in any country or city in the world.

wonder worker 6

Dr. Heal Good

An organic health-food expert can assure you that consistent attention to her diet brings with it a guarantee of excellent health. There is also a fringe benefit: protection from physical harm during your entire life.

7

wonder worker

Professor I. Q. Smartico
This person can bestow the technical skills and know-how to increase your intelligence quotient to whatever you desire, even beyond 155! Once established, this IQ will be permanent as long as you live.

8

wonder worker

D. Gawl Stone
An internationally renowned diplomat and leader is available to teach you all the leadership qualities you need. People the world over will look up to you and seek your advice; you will be respected and admired by everyone.

9

wonder worker

I. M. Popular
This warm soul knows everything about "how to make friends and influence people" and guarantees that you will have any and all the friends you wish. You will have great confidence in relating to these people and they will, in turn, find you easy to approach and comfortable to be with.

10

wonder worker

G. M. Ford
This tycoon has a natural genius that enables him "to succeed in business without really trying." Almost instant wealth will be yours within days. You will have millions of dollars to use without fear of failure--ever.

11

wonder worker

Cell Ebritee
She will give you whatever you need to become a famous actor, dancer, and singer. You will be one of the most sought-after TV and movie personalities in history.

12

wonder worker

U. C. Thinges
She has an uncanny intuitive sense regarding the future. She will tell you anything you want to know about the future of your life and the world. Always available for consultation, 100 percent accuracy.

wonder worker **13** Professor Inn R. Search
A highly respected psychologist and counselor will assist you in truly understanding yourself. The results will give you great self-confidence, a sense of self-worth, and a profound satisfaction in life.

wonder worker **14** Professor Claire Ituppe
Here is a values clarification authority who can give you the skills and techniques you need to clarify and understand any issue that may be complex and confusing. You will know exactly what you want, know why you want it, and experience the satisfying result of obtaining it.

Now that you have selected your *Wonder Workers*, think about those you have chosen. What qualities seem to link together the five most desirable people? What qualities join the five least desirable people? What personal values are indicated by your choices? Do some choices seem out of place with others in a particular group you selected?

The meaning of this strategy is that all of us, in our own ways, with our own talents, are *Wonder Workers*. Our talents may <u>not</u> be 100 percent effective, but they are definite assets to help ourselves and to help others. It is important to recognize these talents. What abilities do you have that could help you achieve what your top five *Wonder Workers* promised to do for you? Refer to your *Values Journal* and make a few notations. What could you do to make your life more "wonder-filled"?

An earlier version of this strategy was developed by and used with the permission of Mark Phillips, University of California at Santa Barbara.

74

Baker's dozen

The baker's dozen used to mean one less than 12, rather than one more. Historically the baker was known for his stingy measure until some harsh medieval laws forced him to mend his ways. Rather than risk having his hand cut off, the baker's parsimony gave way to generous measure.

Baker's Dozen is a strategy of measurement that gets very close to home, even if it isn't centered in the kitchen. Think about the appliances that you use fairly frequently. They can be anything from electric hair dryers to irons, blenders, or mixers.

This could be called an Energy Saving Strategy, considering the "current" emphasis on energy conservation, but it really has other purposes. It stresses a number of value-defining standards: freely choosing from alternatives or from a number of choices; weighing the cost of our choice; prizing and cherishing; and publicly affirming what we believe. To make some sense out of the confusing array of choices in our lives, including the bewildering variety of commercial offerings, we have to set some priorities.

Make a list of 13 electrical appliances that you frequently use. Then draw a line through the three things that you could most easily live without.

75

What if you had to eliminate five more electrical appliances, which five could you next give up most easily? Cross out these five things.

Then asterisk the five things that you think are most important and valuable. These five items would probably represent those things that you would relinquish last.

Now rank in order of importance the five appliances you would keep the longest. If you had to live by this priority, could you?

When you rank appliances or anything "you couldn't live without," you get to the bare bones of your reliance on things. How dependent are you on mechanical gimmicks? How many are really necessary, how many are conveniences, luxuries, and just trivial status symbols?

The importance of this strategy goes beyond electrical appliances. Make a *Baker's Dozen* list of television programs, cooking and laundry products, articles of clothing, books, etc.

What can you live without?
What can't you live without?
And why not?

Madison Avenue

Madison Avenue is as well known as Broadway or Main Street. More than an actual place, it has become a famous (or is it notorious) frame of reference. Madison Avenue is for many people synonymous with glossy advertising agencies, promises, flak, puffery, and commercial hustle-and-sell of the hard or soft variety. And Madison Avenue means brand names.

All too often we become lazy in our buying patterns. Perhaps it is about time to really examine those patterns. Values clarification encourages us to be consciously selective in the choices we make, so that in the process of buying products or of choosing values, we will be more knowledgeable.

The practical aspect of this values clarification strategy is to encourage you to avoid impulse buying, a necessary caution in this time of runaway inflation. Go to the store with a list. Think about what you really need before you make that list. And in the store, stick to that list. Simple? Not so simple!

Madison Avenue asks you to look at your own and your family's pattern of buying, to see how many of the value processes go into each choice.

First of all, go to your medicine cabinet. Make a list similar to the one illustrated below. List items from 1 to 10. Then to the right, make four columns marked I, II, III, and IV. From 1 to 10, list all the brand names in your medicine cabinet. If there are more than ten brand names, your list should allow for the actual number.

	I	II	III	IV
Brand names in my medicine cabinet				
1. *Pep uldard*				
2. *that lurm*				
3.				
4.				
5.				
6.				
7				

In column I, who selected that particular brand? Write the name of the family member or person who bought it.

In column II, give reasons why you think that particular brand was selected. Begin with the products you purchased. What motivated you to buy them? Did a friend recommend them? Did you read about the items in a magazine or newspaper advertisement? Did you see them advertised on TV? After you have answered these questions about the products you have purchased, you might ask others in the family about the products they buy. What makes them select a particular brand? Try to find some reason for each item on your list.

In column III, place a check mark if the product was selected by utilizing each of these three standards.

1 It was selected after examining several choices.
2 It was selected after carefully considering negative and positive aspects.
3 It was selected by free choice, not under pressure.

Brand names in my medicine cabinet	I	II	III	IV
			✓	R
	me	TV		B
1. Papodent	Dad	ad		
2. Ouflam				
3.				
4.				
5.				
6.				
7.				
8.				
9.				
10.				

A fourth column could be added if you wish. Here you might express your feelings by use of the following codes.

➤ B I'll continue buying it, can't bear to live without it.
➤ S I'll stop buying it and keep it off my list.
➤ T I'll transfer my loyalty to another brand name.
➤ R I'll rethink my present buying habit regarding this product.

Some of the products that you purchase may seem to indicate a gullibility. We are all gullible to the Madison Avenue product push, but we can stand on our own much more if we use the standards of values clarification when we purchase anything. Consider the reasons why we may be vulnerable to the enticements of ads and commercials. Do we really need all this stuff to be happy?

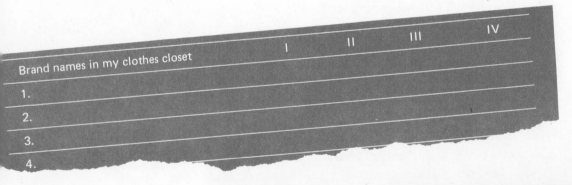

Brand names in my clothes closet	I	II	III	IV
1.				
2.				
3.				
4.				

Brand names in my kitchen	I	II	III
1.			
2.			
3.			
4.			

What's in my wallet?

> Quickly! Without any preconceived notion as to what this exercise is about, make an inventory of your closest or handiest collection of personal things that say something about you.

> That nearby aggregate of odds-and-ends could be your wallet or your handbag, or if you are at your desk, perhaps the top drawer.

> Make a brief list of everything you find in that wallet, handbag, or desk drawer. Code these items P for Past,
Pr for Present,
and F for Future.

Anything that you code P no longer has a use to you. In this category are an expired license or credit card, a faded photograph of someone who <u>was</u> important, an unnecessary receipt. While you're at it, since this is a practical exercise, you might want to throw away some of the P items. Why clutter up your wallet or your life with things of past use or value? On the other hand, some things are too precious to throw away. I have a file folder called Memories. That's where my tender items from the past go.

Code anything Pr that has current use. Examples might be keys, active charge cards, postage stamps, photographs of meaningful people (present or past), useful names and addresses.

What about F? How many items do you have in your wallet, handbag, or desk drawer that fall into that third category—that are directed to the future? Perhaps tickets to a play, concert, or sports event? Maybe a list of films that you want to see? Or restaurants that you might want to try?

Now—how many things that you've just examined, aside from identification cards, say who you are and what kind of person you are? How many things say something personal about you? How many items indicate that you are thinking about the future?

Of course, there are no right or wrong answers. But like many of the inventories in this book, *What's in My Wallet?* says something about what's in your life. Sometimes we need to do something about what we value. Sometimes what we do says more about what we value than what we say. My wallet says a lot about me and what I do, what I value.

coat of arms

In these socially democratic United States, personal coats of arms have never been popular. Historically they have come to represent the old order of inherited power or privilege. Of course, there is an old order of power and privilege in the United States, but it prefers not to flaunt its position by displaying a family crest. Most of us are familiar with these heraldic devices through historical reference or through their use as corporate insignias for automobiles and other products that need a touch of class.

The *Coat of Arms* that this strategy refers to is not concerned with the inherited heraldry of family hand-me-down symbols. The *Coat of Arms* you are asked to draw here is one representing those desirable qualities with which you would like to be associated.

Coat of Arms is a group strategy. It can be an evening's highpoint when five or six people get together to draw and compare their own *Coats of Arms*.

On a large piece of paper or shirt cardboard, copy the *Coat of Arms* illustrated on this page. In the appropriate areas of your *Coat of Arms,* answer the questions on the following page not in words but in pictures.

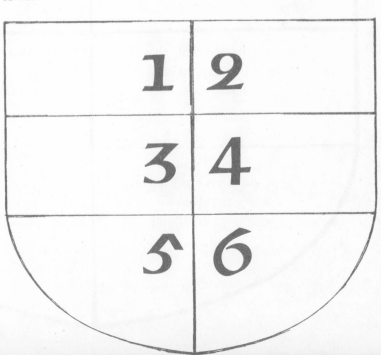

The drawings may be simple, even crude, as long as they mean something to you; as long as you know what they express. This strategy seeks the quality of values, not the quality of artwork.

Why symbols? Not only are symbols or pictographs the traditional means of illustrating heraldic shields, but the use of abstract symbols may force us to think beyond words. As a famous French writer said, "Many of us use words to conceal thought more than to express it." Here we will avoid being too verbal and hiding behind words. Let's see what we can picture.

These are the questions relating to your *Coat of Arms*.

1 What do you regard as your greatest personal achievement?	**2** What do you regard as your family's greatest achievement?
3 What is the one thing that other people can do to make you most happy?	**4** What do you regard as your own greatest personal failure?
5 What would you do if you had one year to live and were guaranteed success in whatever you attempted?	**6** What three words would you most like to have said about you if you died today?

Here's a variation.

1 What is something you are very good at? What is something you are struggling to get better at? Draw two pictures.

2 What is one value, a deep commitment, from which you would never budge?

3 What is the material possession most significant to you?

4 What is your greatest achievement of the past year? What is your biggest setback, failure, or defeat of the past year? Draw two pictures.

5 What would you do with your life if you had it to live over?

6 What three words (qualities) would you like to have associated with you? These could become your personal motto, words to live by.

Keep these questions in mind as you complete the strategy. Do I see my life just as a matter of reaction to others, to outside events? Am I doing what I can to control my life? To make it what I want it to be? How can I get more out of my life?

This is another one of those strategies that can really liven up a social evening. Prepare outlines of the *Coat of Arms* for as many guests as you have invited. Get together a number of magic markers of all colors. Then lead the people through the exercise, one block at a time. I promise the discussion that follows will make one of the most tender and compassionate and alive evenings you've ever had in your home.

Circles of privacy

Circles is a very private strategy that asks, "Are you open?" "Are you closed?" "To what degree?" It will also help determine how properly private or how shy a person you are. Done with friends, it will open up some juicy issues for spirited discussion.

One of the seven processes of values clarification is the one that encourages us to publicly affirm a position or a belief. This affirmation should always be made when the circumstances demand that kind of courage. But when do the circumstances demand? When is it appropriate or inappropriate to publicly affirm a belief? The intent of *Circles of Privacy* is to help you define your pattern of openness and closedness.

What are the things that we are willing to share with others? Some things we properly keep to ourselves. These are no one else's business. Other opinions and feelings that we have we would only share with our most intimate friends, perhaps a wife, husband, or a best friend. Other things, less private, we would willingly share with acquaintances, perhaps neighbors or business associates. And then there are certain facets of our lives that are matters of common knowledge. Even strangers might know these things: where we live, what kind of work we do, maybe our favorite books or movies. Everything depends on who knows what.

On a piece of paper, draw five concentric circles, as illustrated on this page, and label them as indicated. The innermost circle would signify *me*; the next circle, *my best friends*; then *friends*; *people I have met*; and finally *people I don't know too well*. Then think of all the people in your life, as many as possible, and list each by initials in the circle space where he/she belongs.

Now here is a set of key words. Many of them are controversial, many will not apply to you personally. But if they did apply to you personally, with whom would you discuss the issues that these words represent?

me

my
best
friends

friends

people
I have met

people
I don't
know
too well

Here are the key words.

stolen something	health	check bounced
religious doubts	cheat on income tax	slapped a child
dislike parents	amount of income tax paid	cost of house
first love	for whom you vote	racial prejudices
something you dislike about your best friends	thoughts of suicide	cried
	smoke pot	jealousy
sexual experiences	use illegal drugs	birth control
salary	had an abortion	discontent with some part of your body
innermost desires	marriage problems	
personal problems		cheated

Perhaps you won't have room in the circle spaces to write these key words. If not, write the words outside the circles with a line extending to the circle spaces where they belong.

This list is only a beginning. Other key words should come easily to mind, or, indeed, be suggested by casually looking through a newspaper.

After completing *Circles of Privacy*, what have you found out about yourself? What does this strategy tell you about your openness, about your closedness? What do you think you've discovered about yourself? You might refer back to the *Discoveries* strategy at this point. Also, it might be a good idea to enter some of these things in your *Values Journal.*

Now that you have found out something about your priority of privacy and how private a person you are, perhaps you would like to compare privacy rankings with a friend. This comparing is a useful exercise if you are both honest, but it is also chancey because in the process of the exercise itself, you might reveal something that you don't want revealed. Or you might stumble upon something about your friend that he or she doesn't want revealed—frankly, something that may be none of your business. However, if two people (three or four for that matter) are willing to play this strategy and to reveal their *Circles of Privacy*, then full speed ahead.

Something to think about: *Circles of Privacy* is a self-inventory and an inventory-of-others. It is one of a number of selection-processes that we employ consciously or unconsciously all the time.

How many of those people you know agree with your opinions and, most importantly, your values? *Circles of Privacy* could be useful in making friends; perhaps it will help you move someone from the *friends* circle to the *my best friends* circle. It would be most desirable, of course, if your privacies matched the privacies of others on each level of closeness, but life isn't always like that. However, it might be a significant error to have a privacy circle very different from that of someone you are close to, or think you are close to. In that case, what is the basis for closeness? And so spins the life-questioning behind values clarification.

Who are all those others?

And what are they doing in my life?

This private strategy can help you recognize who influences your values and to what extent. Who are the significant others in your life, and what do they expect of you? What are you willing to give, to commit yourself to privately or publicly?

On a piece of paper, draw up a chart something like the one illustrated on this page. Identify real people in each of the categories and write their names (or initials) inside the blocks.

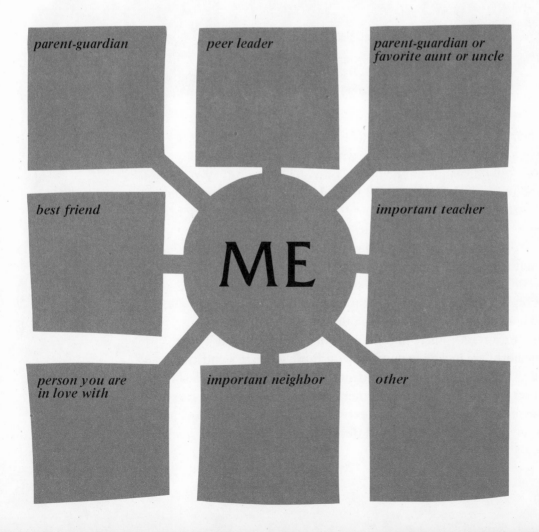

parent-guardian

peer leader

parent-guardian or favorite aunt or uncle

best friend

ME

important teacher

person you are in love with

important neighbor

other

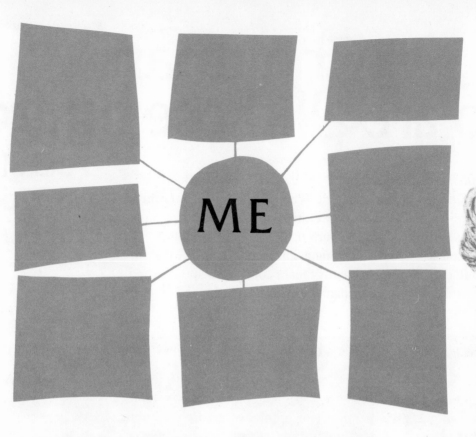

Then list four or five things each of these significant others
<u>want</u> you to value. Essentially, what do they count on you
for? What demands do they place on you? What do they want
you to be, to do, or to think? What do they want you to value?

After you've done that, consider the similarities and differ-
ences between what the various people in your life want from
you. Then, in each block, underline each item that you also
want for yourself. Make a list in the *me* block (or draw a line
to the margin) that restates those things you are willing to
accept as things you also want for yourself. These are the beliefs
to hold dear. And for the ones others want of you that you
don't want? Ah, there in bold print one can often find where
the horns are locked in conflict with those who are significant
to us. Negotiation is the word from there. We may need to say
clearly what <u>we</u> want. Or tell them with as much gentleness as
possible, "No." Perhaps the next strategy will help, too. As one
of my children used to say, "Life ain't no ride on no pink duck."

Chairman of the board

Are you *Chairman of the Board* of your own life? If your life were a large corporation, who would be sitting in the Chairman's seat? And who would be the other Directors on your Board?

Of course, this strategy doesn't ask you to assume that your life is a business corporation. It <u>does</u> ask you to select in a businesslike way the Directors of your life.

Even more than the last strategy, *Who Are All Those Others?*, this one asks you to <u>remove</u> certain Directors from your Board of Life, those who give continually negative or even destructive advice. Perhaps others should be awarded those seats on your Board.

To begin this rather private strategy, draw a board table (a large rectangle), then draw or suggest chairs around this table. How many chairs depends on the number of Directors in your life who have a stake in a <u>particular</u> decision to be made or a problem to be solved. Perhaps there are six, perhaps more—10 or 12, depending on the particular action before the Board.

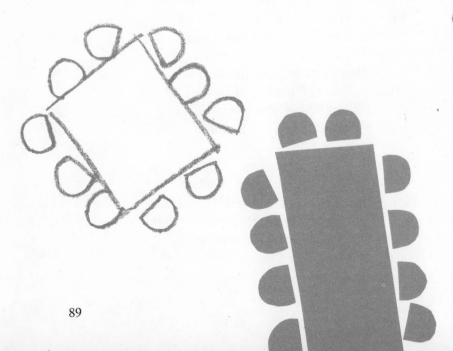

more ▶

Let's assume there is a specific issue before the Board, a problem in your life, a decision to be made. Perhaps it is a change of job, a question of your relationship with someone else, a confusing problem involving your children. Perhaps it is a question of publicly affirming a particular belief. Whatever it is (and you select it), that is the question before your Board of Directors. It will, of course, determine the number of Directors on your Board and who they are.

Once you know the number and the names of your Board members in relation to the particular problem to be solved, write their initials next to their chairs. Then make brief notes about the kind of advice you think they would give. Do they listen with an open mind? Do they consider all factors fairly? Or do they give advice only from their standpoint based on their values?

If you are your own *Chairman of the Board*, you should know the nature of their advice and appreciate their decision-making processes sympathetically and realistically. (Sometimes as a knowledgeable Chairman, you can't and shouldn't kick certain of these people off your Board of Directors. Their position is of great importance to them. Or they have a right to be there and give advice. Other members on the Board of Life are there because they possess authority, and we have to recognize that.) The main thing is: whose advice is more important? Why? What is the relationship of your Board of Directors to you?

You should be aware of your own decision-making processes, even if you can't completely control the direction of all decisions. Try to be your own *Chairman of the Board*. Unless you are in control and can make a decision, freely chosen (even with the advice of others), you will not have achieved something valuable. And someone else will sit in the Chairman's seat making value judgments for you.

Telegrams for action

There is a principle of the Gestalt school of psychology that says everything we want for someone else, we really want for ourselves. *Telegrams for Action* takes note of this projection-principle: it is others directed while publicly affirming a belief that we, ourselves, prize.

The two parts of *Telegrams for Action* provide a simple means by which you can clearly and concisely state beliefs that are important to you. They are the personal practice part and the personal action part.

Take several 3 x 5 cards or, better, obtain a pad of blank Western Union telegraph forms. Choose five real people and write telegrams to those people beginning with these words, "I urge that you . . . ." The message is to consist of 15 words or less, and you are to sign your name to this practice telegram.

The five people to whom you write these practice telegrams should be a mixture of public figures and personal contacts. For example, think of a political issue that interests you. Perhaps an important piece of legislation is before the Senate or the House of Representatives. You might want to write your congressman urging action one way or the other.

Or you might want to telegraph advice to friends or relatives who need encouragement. Write them your "I urge . . ." endorsement. In every case, the telegram should reflect something that you feel is important, something that you hold dear.

What is the most pressing issue in your life at this time, an issue that calls for decision? On the last telegram form, after having written five urgings to others, write a practice telegram to yourself. In 15 words or less, what would you say, what action would you advise that you take?

Remember, every time you make a decision, every time you urge yourself or others toward a value-affirmation or decision, you must accept the responsibility for your action. You have to assume that obligation if your decision is to have value.

With this in mind, consider taking personal action: why not actually send a telegram to someone close to you who is wavering on the brink of a decision. Maybe it is a friend or relative who is thinking about giving up smoking. Your thoughtful telegram, "I urge that you give up smoking. Friends who love you want you to live," might give that person courage to make the decision.

In *Telegrams for Action*, you are putting yourself on the line, and you should not hesitate to do so, <u>but</u> only after weighing the consequences. What is the nature of your urging or advice? Does it violate someone's privacy? Does the intensity of your friendship with that person warrant the invasion of privacy? Will that person, not you, be the primary beneficiary of your advice? (*Telegrams for Action* is <u>not</u> an exercise in ego-satisfaction.) If these vital signs say, "go ahead," then don't waver: send your "I urge . . ." telegram.

But remember, the quality of caring, like the quality of mercy,

> *is not strain'd.*
> *It droppeth as the gentle rain from heaven*
> *Upon the place beneath: it is twice blest:*
> *It blesseth him that gives and him that takes.*

Your advice or urging should be gentle and caring and truly reflect <u>charm</u> as defined by the great French aphorist Amiel, "the quality in others of making us more satisfied with ourselves."

Magical mystery boxes

In its wish-fulfillment potential, the *Magical Mystery Boxes* strategy recalls The Beatles' "Magical Mystery Tour," a wish-fulfillment pop-rock number of the late 1960s. But the content of these *Magical Mystery Boxes* depends on your personal projection of what might be. This is a gentle little strategy to be played with your family or friends, perhaps at the dinner table.

What we wish says something about what we value. You can have three different *Magical Mystery Boxes*, one very small, one medium sized, and one as large as you want it to be. Best of all, they can contain anything that you want them to contain.

What would be in your *Magical Mystery Boxes*? Something tangible? Intangible? Before determining the contents, you might ask yourself, "What do I find the most valuable?" It might be something significant but small, even whimsical. For example, what is the smallest tangible thing you might want? What is the smallest intangible thing you might want? Follow with decisions on the contents of the medium and the large-as-you-want *Magical Mystery Boxes*.

WISH

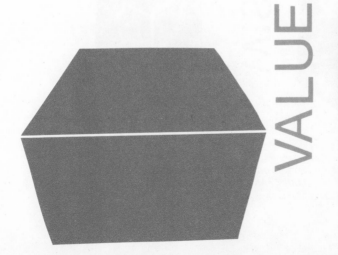

VALUE

VALUE

After you have decided what all the *Magical Mystery Boxes* should contain for yourself, think, "What might they contain for my husband/wife or family? My best friend or a very good friend? (The same sense of 'wonder' should prevail.) The smallest thing? A silly but appropriate (to that person) thing?"

Now you might rank order (see the *Priorities* strategy, pages 44-53) the contents of your *Magical Mystery Boxes* in various categories—for yourself, for others.

What have you been doing or what could you be doing to attain the tangible or intangible contents of the *Magical Mystery Boxes* in your life?

Assume the role of a value-direction leader. Play the game with your family or friends. What do their *Magical Mystery Boxes* wishes mean to them? What are we saying to each other about all our needs? How can we make life a banquet as Auntie Mame suggests?

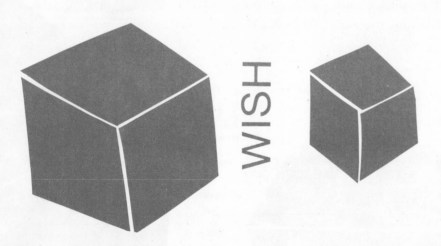

WISH

A variation of this strategy was once learned from Jack Canfield, Director of the New England Center for Personal and Organizational Development, Amherst, Massachusetts.

94

a christmas gift of love

Unfortunately, the Christmas season is all too often a time of greedy scratching for presents. Gimme. Buy me. Get me.

Of course, it could be, "What did I give?" The spirit of Christmas, even beyond its particular religious significance, often truly means giving and sharing and getting in return. These are not necessarily material gifts, but giving the gift of oneself and experiencing the love of friends.

A Christmas Gift of Love need not be limited to the yuletide calendar. It's useful throughout the year in helping us look at the way we give gifts. Take a piece of paper and divide it into four columns from top to bottom. In the first, list the five friends who are closest to you. Then list three to five members of your family who are very close to you. In the second column, list the gifts you gave to those people last Christmas or the gifts you think you will give them this Christmas. These should be actual material gifts.

In the third column, list a gift of the spirit that you might give to each of these people. This gift would be a special quality, such as love, kindness, or patience, that would most help that particular person in his quest for a better life. Give each of these eight to ten people a carefully chosen intangible gift that you believe would make that person happier.

In the fourth column, list the gift that each of these people might give you, something you think <u>they</u> might feel you need based on their close knowledge of you. What quality would each of these people like to see you have? Maybe their gifts of behavioral or personality change would be similar. If so, it might tell you something useful about yourself, your friends, and your relationships with them.

You can help other people achieve their goals by giving them what you think they would want, but most importantly, you can help them achieve their goals by giving them the year-round gift of love: friendship. In a sense, that is the ultimate value.

friends and family	things	spirit	rec'd

95

I resolve...

Why is it that resolutions always seem to be made on what we Americans know as New Year's Day? On our Western (or Gregorian) calendar, that date means January 1. A very limiting date.

Remember that new years start for many other people on different and differing dates. The Chinese, the Moslems, the Jews, all whose calendars have a certain historic fidelity and seasonal continuity, begin their New Year (and their New Year's Day resolutions) on moveable feasts. The point is—and the point of this strategy is: let's make New Year's Resolutions whenever we are prepared to resolve. It could be on anybody's New Year's Day or on any day. It could mean a new or better life.

I Resolve... depends on much that has gone before. Refer to your *Values Journal* notations. What do your *Discoveries* tell you about yourself?

What resolutions are you willing to make, able to make?

Everyone wants his or her resolutions to stick; everyone starts with such good intentions, but so often there's a slip 'twixt the promise and the practice.

Here's a method of ranking resolutions that will help you grade them on a personal-gain basis. Take a piece of paper and divide it into three vertical columns. In the first column list all the resolutions you have made, or plan to make, or need to make. All of them—or as many as you can think of, past, present, and future. Your resolutions may include a change in behavior, something you wish to learn, a new skill you might want to acquire, or new ways of getting along better with other people, etc.

In the second column, briefly list what you think you will gain if the resolution in the first column is accomplished. In what way will your life be better? At this point, it might be a good idea to get together with someone you trust and ask his

all my resolutions	what I will gain	five most valued
[handwritten, illegible]	*[handwritten, illegible]*	

or her help in completing the second column. Naturally, you would help that person fill his second column, too.

The next step is to look at the resolutions you value the most, as well as the resolutions that would not be a total loss if they weren't put into action.

In the third column, renumber your resolutions. Rank them until you have identified the five most valued resolutions.

Now intently look at these five resolutions. Ask yourself, as you read each one, "Is this pie-in-the-sky that will never come true?"

Finally, circle the resolutions—one, two, or five—that are really achievable.

Now turn to the next strategy.

Contracts with myself

You should now have a limited number of *I Resolve(s)*...
determined as achievable and based on everything you now
know about yourself. After working through these strategies
and the processes of values clarification: Act!

Contracts with Myself is an action strategy. It will help you
put theory into practice, help you know and get what you want.
It concerns those things that are realistic and achievable.

Following the now familiar values clarification method of
putting it in writing, a self-contract is a formal document, signed
and dated by you. Additionally, it is signed by your contract
holder, a trusted friend.

On the next page, you can see the form that your resolution-
contract should take.

Contracts with Myself are similar to self-resolutions in that
they should be simple, direct, and possible. On your resolution-
contract due date (it might be three or six months hence), get
together with your contract holder for a contract-burning
celebration that will honor the fulfillment of your obligation.

Good luck on fulfilling your contract, not only up to the due
date but beyond that, throughout the many days of your life.

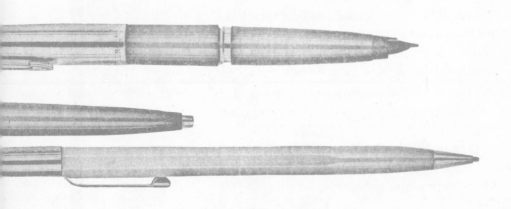

I

_____
your name

make this contract
that by

_____
due date

I will live by the following resolution:

_____

_____

_____

I will give a copy of this to

_____
name of contract holder

who will contact me by the due date to celebrate with me the completion

of this contract and at which time we will have a contract burning.

_____
your signature   signature of contract holder

99

EPITAPH

Conclude your values clarification strategies as you began, with a postscript reminder of mortality. This time let it be an epitaph.

But before you write your post-values clarification *Epitaph*, you'll want to refer to your original pre-values clarification "Obituary Notice." Also, since this is a good time for review, reread the seven standards of values clarification as chronicled in your *Values Chart*. Other strategies you will especially want to review are your *Discoveries*, *Data Diary* and/or *Reflections*, and *Values Journal*.

Epitaph: following the example of the inscriptions on old tombstones, complete this line in 15 words or less. "Here lies . . . ."

Your *Epitaph* should represent the fullness of your burgeoning search for values clarification and the new knowledge that you have of yourself. Reflecting this self-knowledge, how would you write your *Epitaph*? How would it read now?

The author of this book would like to be remembered this way.

HERE LIES

Sid Simon—

searcher, teacher, giver.

And needing, wanting, loving,

and sometimes crying.

AUTHOR'S POST NOTE

As you have seen, the processes of values clarification are a serious, purposeful method. But just as the strategies in this book began and ended on a slightly somber note—death, only to show the vitality of life in perspective, so values clarification itself is only a means toward the end that life is too short not to live it to the fullest and to joyfully share it! Knowing, giving, and getting.

And that is the essential purpose of values clarification: to freely choose values; to vivaciously cherish them; to vitally affirm them; and to positively act on those values. It is values that give life zest and meaning. That is our simple moral.

Values clarification as a method of learning began in the classroom with children. It was children who first grasped, and perhaps, still understand best, the liveliness, the playfulness of the values clarification search. Their *Who Am I . . . ?* seeking is always touched with humor, a sense of irony, and a childlike detachment from phony adult self-importance.

It would be wise to emulate them: don't take yourself too seriously. Know yourself, but know yourself with the guilelessness of children. As you work and play, the *Who Am I . . . ?* self-adventure should become an artless touchstone for living. From knowing yourself, your behaviors and your patterns, a new confidence, an internal security, and a sense of potency will emerge that is life-giving. And that is the true meaning of values clarification, to keep the vital juices of life flowing. As you meet yourself halfway, may you go the whole way with joy and delight.

Dr. Sidney B. Simon conducts weekend workshops in values
clarification in many major cities in the country. If you would
like to receive an announcement, and be put on the mailing list,
please send a self-addressed, stamped #10 envelope to:

Dr. Sidney B. Simon
Box 846
Leverett, Mass. 01054